THE POLITICAL INJUSTICE AFFECTING OUR SCHOOLS, TEACHERS AND STUDENTS

THE POLITICAL INJUSTICE AFFECTING OUR SCHOOLS, TEACHERS AND STUDENTS

Dr. G.V. Hair

To order additional copies of this book, contact:
Xlibris Corporation
1-888-795-4274
www.Xlibris.com
Orders@Xlibris.com

To my wife Cindy and my daughter Abigail,
you two are what inspires me.

INTRODUCTION

As I wrote this book I began to realize there were three main reasons for its creation. Two of the reasons are for my own self-benefit and the last reason is to show support and help anyone who reads this book to understand that our educational system and teachers have not ever failed our students. The book is written from my point of view as an educator for thirty-three years and reflects all the observations and conclusions I have formed. I would also like to point out that I am a true classroom teacher. I started in the classroom and I will finish my career in the classroom. I am not like other individuals who spend at most five years in the classroom and call themselves experts. I do not consider myself an expert in education because as a classroom teacher I am always learning. I do consider myself an experienced educator.

The first self-benefit for me in writing the book allowed me to vent the anger that I had stored up for the last fifteen years of my career as a teacher. The public does not realize how frustrated teachers (me in particular) have become since the standardization of education by our politicians. When the creative aspect of your job is constantly being taken away little by little year after year, disappointment develops into resentment and resentment develops into anger. Through the last fifteen or so years I have seen teaching go from a creative, independent profession to a standardized assembly line type of job. Politicians and district noneducational personnel have literally taken 90 percent of a teacher's ability to be inventive and creative in the classroom. They have standardized the professional practice of teaching. The individuals making the decisions in education have no background in education other than the years they were in the classroom as a student and I am not real sure that any of them actively performed well as a student in school. The politicians and noneducational district personnel have dismantled education and now control everything a student is to learn in their educational career. Their interest in educational issues is timed only when they feel threatened to lose their jobs. Their decisions are based solely on financial commitments they made to their contributors and are not based on what is best for our children. When have you ever seen a politician or a high-ranking district administrator spend more than a handshake in a public school? And we are allowing these individuals to make the decisions for our children's education.

Second, every hour that I wrote gave me more time to reflect and organize my thoughts. These thoughts have developed through many years of observing individuals with no or limited educational backgrounds who believe they know what is best for education in America; seeing so many times money and time wasted on programs and professional development that did little to help teachers in the classroom help their students; seeing how the whole attitude toward a moral, disciplined education has taken a backseat to a compromised education—thoughts I am sure a lot of other teachers in this great country continue to feel every day. I hope the final product that you are about to read is organized in an understandable format for both educators and noneducators. This is especially important for noneducators as I hope to help them understand why educational experience is important. I hope individuals with little or no background in education will begin to respect our teachers for the job they do. I hope to help everyone understand that teaching is not a profession anyone can perform. It takes time and experience to become a true educator and it is a constant learning and developmental process. It is a profession that needs freedom and creativity in what we teach, how we teach, and how we assess what is learned. I have organized the chapters to reflect the domino effect that has resulted from the time we all were first led to believe our students were falling behind the rest of the students in the world.

My final reason for writing this book deals with years of watching politicians and the media continually use education and teachers as a means of blame for governmental financial abuse. Through all my years in education, I have never seen teacher morale at such a low point. I am here to tell you our educational system was never lacking in quality and our teachers are and continue to be the best in the world. I really feel politicians have developed this whole process of bashing teachers and our American educational system for several reasons.

Politicians realized at some point in the late 1970s and early 1980s that if they could scare the public into thinking our educational system and our teachers were failing our students, then the politicians could sell the public on an educational platform and get elected. Politicians knew their voting constituencies were mothers, fathers, grandmothers, and grandfathers, and these individuals had a special interest in the youth of today. Politicians used the media to present half-truths of statistics relating American education to education in other parts of the world. Once the media jumped on board, politicians gained control of what and how education was presented to the public. This has allowed the flow of information concerning education to be selective and influential in the developing of negative attitudes and lack of confidence in our public educational system and our teachers.

Politicians have taken the control of information on education and influenced the leadership associated with the individual school districts. Politicians have convinced the public that the best leadership for education should have a business approach. As a result, there are multiple positions within any school district occupied by individuals with none to very little educational background. These individuals are making choices that are a financial nightmare to tax dollars, and when the choices are deemed not to work, the blame is always placed on the teachers and their inability to adapt or perform. These are the same individuals who in one breath indicate their concern for issues in education and then turn around in another breath to cut finances or programs because of the bottom dollar. I hope to give you specific examples that support my claim and help to show the real root to the problem that has developed in education.

Politicians have expanded the standardized testing system to a point where it has restricted students from their right to select multiple courses in both academics and the vocational area. Freedom is a word we use strongly in the United States of America, and politicians have made sure our children do not get to exercise their freedom in the selection of courses they can learn from. I feel there is an underlying agenda in which politicians would like to produce a student who cannot think for themselves and have to be told what to do and how to do it. How easy would it be for politicians to rule in whatever capacity they feel with individuals who have been standardized?

The main threat to our politicians in their standardizing agenda is the experienced teachers and administrators who have the past years of involvement in education to compare and see all the bad decisions being made in education. Politicians with the media's help have created a campaign against the experienced teachers and educational administrators. They use tactics such as constantly mentioning how incompetent teachers with many years of experience use that experience to protect themselves from being fired and never mentioning how really low the percentage of bad experience is. This gives the public the impression that all experienced teachers are incompetent. Politicians have completely misrepresented the idea of a pension in the case of teachers, law-enforcement, and firemen, all the while never bringing the pension and the benefits they receive out into the open.

Politicians have year after year for a long time cut the funding for extracurricular activities and even have gone as far as to cut certain extracurricular programs completely from the educational system. It amazes me how we have let our politicians fund our tax dollars to some for-profit organizations while cutting the funding to our schools. And the first programs to suffer from any type of decrease in funding are the extracurricular activities. Our schools—the extracurricular activities at our schools—and the classroom should not suffer because there is plenty of funds available if the tax dollars are not used as paybacks by our politicians.

The standardized movement has produced a particularly interesting effect on the parents of our students. No longer are parents talking to their children and asking what their plans are in life. No longer are parents checking and making sure their children are truly understanding what they are studying. It appears that parents are satisfied with their children receiving a passing grade on a standardized test. In short, I do not think a lot of parents really know what their children are interested in and what their children truly want to be when they grow up. Technology has made parenting a lazy job. Parents can put their children in front of a computer, an I-phone, or an I-pad and not be bothered with entertaining their children. Technology has made it easy for parents to check on the progress or results of their children in their classes or extracurricular activities never really having to make physical contact. Parents have allowed politicians to fool them into thinking there is a shortage of funding and programs at school should suffer or be cut. This has presented additional financial commitments to parents outside the public school system. I think parents have fallen into this hole of bad habits because of our political mandates and have been blinded to see the truth.

Teachers and academic administrators all across this country are taking the fall for a lot of the countries problems. Politicians are using negative publicity about different aspects of the teaching profession and making sure support for teachers both financially and academically is a hard thing to come. There have been attacks on the retirement system of teachers and the amount of money that is a cost to taxpayers. There have been different organizations (supported by politicians) formed to supposedly train individuals to be master teachers in place of support for teachers to obtain higher level academic degrees. Politicians have sold the public on a lottery system that was supposed to enhance our educational budget not substitute money in the budget so politicians could take the substituted funds and use it for their contributors. Everything I mentioned above are topics I attempt to explain in this book. I hope that as you read this book there are issues I open your eyes to and they give you a sense of urgency to help change our politician's ways. I truly believe what has made this country great is the idea of freedom and our children's freedoms are slowly being dissolved through the standardization of our educational system.

CHAPTER 1

POLITICIANS AND THE MEDIA

I CANNOT GIVE YOU AN exact date or time at which politicians realized that the key to getting elected and staying elected was controlling the public educational system, but it did happen and it is still happening today. Politicians are using our educational system to standardize our children and make our children unable to think for themselves. This in turn allows our politicians to control the information given to the public without being held accountable. This whole process of controlling education started in the 1970s and has reached a very alarming situation that needs to be changed.

Let's start with the famous SAT score decline of the early 1970s. Politicians and the media were quick to jump when they saw that the average SAT score for our public school students was declining in the 60s and 70s. For more than a decade, the American public has repeatedly been informed that our educational system failed our children and educationally we have fallen behind the world. The old bad news is the news cliché in our media circus. Politicians used the media to scare the nation into thinking American students were falling behind the rest of the world in their academics and our nation was becoming less of an economic power in the world. Politicians saw a way to have the public perceive them as concerned and caring about

America's educational future. They placed the blame on the schools and the teachers claiming both had to be held accountable. Politicians wanted the public to believe they were the savior that would bring America out of the educational darkness to once again be at the top of the world in academic achievement. The problem with this whole myth is that only a fraction of the story was presented and lurking variables associated with the statistics were never presented and explained to the public. Politicians and the media chose to use selective information for political interests. At the present date, politicians are still using this myth as a political agenda for election and in the process of using the myth, politicians have dismantled an educational system that was a solid and productive machine. Let's look at some points that need to be considered in dispelling the myth.

American education is free education to anyone who resides in this country. We are a country that welcomes all races, cultures, and religions into our educational system. An education in America is a right that every individual has. For other countries in this world, education is a privilege or benefit that is earned through governmental appointment. The sixties and early seventies brought about great social changes in our society and these societal changes brought about numerous educational changes. In education, minorities and low socioeconomic students were given greater opportunities to pursue postsecondary educations. Please do not confuse the term low socioeconomic with color of skin because there are a good number of white families then and now in this category. This in turn increased the amount of minorities and low socioeconomic students taking the SAT, which resulted in a lower average score. This statement is not made to place blame on minorities and low socioeconomic level students but to emphasize the point of the significant gain our society made in the educational process of education to all. About half of the decline on the SAT between 1960 and 1990 can be attributed to the fact that the test was taken by proportionately fewer students in the top 20 percent of their graduating class and proportionately more students in the lower 60 percent. It seems to me that if we are truly a democratic nation, then this point alone should be one that is not emphasized but embraced by our political leaders. The fact that the top 20 percent declined is not cause for alarm because the decline can be attributed to a number of reasons such as the introduction of another standardized test, the ACT. Now if you think about this aforementioned information, this is a very positive statistic because it gives proof of how America's educational system has advanced to help more students achieve goals of attending higher academic institutions. More students who are non-U.S. citizens or who report English is not their primary language are taking the SAT. In this country we do not limit an individual student's right to education or the ability to take the SAT based on race, creed, color, or religion. This in itself shows one reason for decreasing scores due to the possible language barriers. These are all factors that correlate with lower test scores across a wide spectrum of measures (Sandia Report, 1993; Stedman, 1994). Politicians and the media chose to report the declining score but not the fact that there was an increase in minorities and low socioeconomic students now entering into postsecondary education. It would appear that the media and our politicians do not consider allowing more individuals to pursue a higher level of education an important progression in our educational system. In fact the quality of education in our public schools had not declined at all; one might say the education a child was receiving had actually improved to benefit more of the overall student population then ever before.

In 1941, SAT was normed and 6.68 percent of the students taking the test scored above a 650. The number of minority and low socioeconomic students taking the test in 1941 was a very small percentage. Through the years the proportion of high scorers has increased 65 percent despite the fact that a considerably larger proportion of test takers came from groups that have consistently scored lower than the elite group on which the test was originally normed (Bracey, 1994). This is a significant piece of statistics showing how the educational system in America has not only improved test scores but also created an improvement on test scores through the whole student population. Why have the media and the politicians neglected to emphasize this information? The fact that the American educational system is not only preparing more minorities and low socioeconomic students to take the SAT and pursue a college degree deserves kudos within itself, but to add to this that the proportion of high-scoring students has increased is icing on the cake. The Educational Testing Service is the organization that develops the SAT test and they have admitted that the test of today is considerably more difficult than the test given in 1975 (Berlinger, 1992, citing the 1991 draft of the Sandia Report). Wow! Imagine that not only do we have these positive points to consider, but now we learn that the test is considerably harder. So let's think about this: the American educational system has improved the amount of minorities and low socioeconomic students taking the test, the American educational system has increased the amount of high scorers on the test, and the organization producing the test admits that the test itself has increased in difficulty. In reference to poor SAT scores and how our schools are failing us, I think it is clear that certain key bits of information were not reported to the public. This information not only would have helped the public to see that the decrease in test scores was a result of a positive change in our educational system, but also helped them understand that by giving the opportunity for higher education to more individuals in our country, we strengthen our country. Our school systems were strong academic institutions that were designed to promote a well-rounded education and successfully serve a wide variety of students.

Another part to the important SAT test scores political myth is how the American educational system is compared to other educational systems in the world. When we consider this type of comparison one must consider the fact that a high percent of the nations in this world do not give every child a chance to receive full education.

Most nations weed out the less performing students and educate only the higher performing students. To receive an education in a lot of countries, a student must show his or her value to the governmental powers (this is exactly were we are headed with standardized testing). Over and over we hear how American students rate poorly compared to the rest of the world. This is true only if you pick the very minute negatives of any statistics related to this topic. In fact University of Pennsylvania researchers Erling E. Boe and Sujie Shin looked at six major international tests in reading, mathematics, science, and civics taken during the years 1991 through 2001 and found that Americans were above average when compared with 22 other industrialized nations. This is startling when you consider that the United States has steadily increased in the amount of low-performing students. We have individuals from all over the world bringing their sons and daughters to America to receive a fair education. Actually, American students are improving, or at most holding their own when it comes to being compared to other nations. As a matter of fact, no nation included in the major international rankings educates as many socioeconomically challenged students or culturally diverse a population as the United States. Why aren't these positives being emphasized by our politicians? The reason is really quite simple; politicians create a negative attitude about the school systems and our teachers only to throw attention away from all the amount of money being misused in the political system. Politicians have become masters at manipulating the public into focusing on issues that are of great personal concern so that they are able to hide financial paybacks to their campaign contributors in various bills. It is not uncommon for politicians to cut X millions of dollars from education while at the same time giving businesses X millions of dollars in tax breaks. Politicians seem to observe the profession of education as a minimum wage job and not as a profession designed to help develop our youth into intellectually strong citizens. It appears to me that politicians would like to see the youth of America decrease in their intellectual strengths so as to be dependent on the politicians to make all of their decisions without debate. Imagine being a politician and being able to make the decisions that no one holds you accountable for. This is where we are headed and politicians are not the only ones with a stake in the whole process of standardizing our educational system.

Business leaders have used the education platform to influence the public in a certain political direction. As far back as the Sputnik crisis and even into modern times of the policy manifesto known as "A Nation at Risk," business leaders have warned that the deficiencies in high school graduates have come at a time when the demand for skilled workers is at a premium. Despite these negative reflections on the American educational system, the United States has survived. Today, the Soviet Union is merely a memory and now business leaders and politicians try and use China as the driving force for their hypothetical myths. "Bad or low performing schools," has been the popular phrase for trying to pin the blame on our American educational system for America's declining competitiveness in world trade. We are led to believe this decline is the result of our educational system not preparing our students for success in the business world. Our politicians and business leaders are very good at making sure the media is a tool for expressing this myth. However, the World Economic Forum did not blame America's educational system for the decline, but cited U.S. trade and budget deficits, increased governmental spending, and a low savings rate to name a few as the causes. Where and when was this information given to the public in support of our public educational system? Think about all of the problems we are facing in our economy and what blame falls on our educational system. I believe you come to the conclusion that the educational system in our country has very little blame. Is our educational system the blame for corporations and businesses moving their factories and headquarters to other countries? Is our educational system the blame for all the corruption and greed in the upper administrative positions of our businesses and corporations?

I think the real blame belongs to our supposed public service individuals—our career politicians. Is education responsible for the high rate of un-employment in our country? Again I think the lack of good political decision making has played the major role. Business leaders and politicians have continually used negative myths about America's educational system to try and cover up for the real reasons on our declining competitiveness in world trade.

State politicians and state media all across the country have continually told the public that our public schools are low performing and need to be held accountable for the education a student receives. They have convinced the public into thinking that if a student passes a standardized test, it is an accurate indication of the knowledge and the potential the student has academically. One day, one test is an indication of what a student knows educationally for the time that student has spent in the classroom. Politicians then devise some type of mathematical model that takes into account multiple factors from the standardized test scores and based on a numerical scale schools receive a letter grade. The problem with this system is it is not consistent and I have seen in Florida the factors and the scale changes continuously from year to year. Most of the grading that is used in Florida is weighted heavily on the bottom 25 percent of the schools population. What this means in Florida is a school could have enough points on the scale to be an A school but if the bottom 25 percent do not show enough improvement, the school letter grade can be dropped one- possibly two-letter grades. This is especially devastating to a school with a grade of C because dropping one- or two-letter grades places the school in the D or F category. If you understand what I have just written, then think of where the district is going to spend most of the money to make sure all of their schools receive passing grades. Right, programs are designed to boost the scores of that bottom 25 percent. What about the other 75 percent and what are the state and the district doing for them? Are our politicians now satisfied that the upper 75 percent has demonstrated that they are fully capable educational individuals? I would like to point out a couple of things. First, how can you base students' academic abilities on one test? There are so many factors that are not considered with a standardized test. There are the qualities of motivation, desire, self-discipline, and perseverance. These qualities can only be measured through observation over a period of time. There is the idea of interests; people in general tend to perform better when they are working in an area that they have an interest in. I wonder how many of the bottom 25 percent students would score better on a state standardized test that was geared toward their interests.

One thing I have observed about the timeline on standardized testing and its scoring is how the scoring is adjusted in a political election cycle. It always seems the scores for our schools drop or decrease just after an election. The politicians and the media inform the public that for some reason our students are not performing at a high enough level. They sell the public on the idea that our teachers are not performing in a suitable way and there needs to be changes in the instructional process. As time proceeds to another year the scores still stay somewhat the same with different schools exchanging lower to higher grades and some schools exchanging higher grades to lower grades. When an election year comes into view, the scores for all the schools miraculously go up and there are more high-performing schools than in the years previous to the last election. It is no big secret that the adjustment to the mathematical formula (if there is a mathematical formula) is controlled by the politicians. In my observations, there is always the same pattern from one election cycle to the next. The school scores go down after an election and then the school scores rise up just before the next election. This allows the incumbent politicians to appear as if they have worked hard to improve the education of our children. What people do not understand is while our politicians play this up-and-down cycle from one election to the next, our students are receiving a general standardized education that never advances in expectations. Politicians are using the standardized testing procedure as an influence to gain an advantage during election times.

In all of this standardized test movement we seem to have allowed our politicians to convince us that all students are college bound. We have allowed our politicians to make the decision for our students that they should want to attend college. The politicians are using the idea of every parent's dreams of having their son/daughter eligible to go to college to keep the standardized testing issue alive. The problem is we have a very high percentage of students who really do not or cannot attend college. What are we doing for the students who want to enter into a vocational or trade career? Politicians have played on the emotions of parents who want their children to all be college bound and in the process we have made students who would like to learn a trade or enter into some vocational career feel as if their goals are not good enough. This truly is a sad, sad situation.

It is common political practice now to use our educational system as a scapegoat for personal and political gains. Politicians use education, our schools, and our teachers as a means of creating platforms, which help them to achieve their political goals. Business leaders use education as means to smokescreen the real issues involved with America's problems in the economy and world trade. These individuals are not concerned with reporting all of the facts; they use select statistical information to influence or scare the public into thinking our educational system is broken. They use this same information to gain the public's support on agendas that have standardized our educational system. The amazing thing about this whole situation is whenever there are problems with money at the state and federal levels, there is never any kind of statistics shown to the public about governmental spending as it relates to business. I feel that politicians are bought through campaign monies and are then obligated to make sure the business sector is protected from taxes and is provided with taxpayer money for private means. It is in my opinion that these political and business individuals have a vested interest in making sure our students do not become independent creative thinkers. These individuals would like to see everyone under them become standardized and become dependent upon the government to make all decisions for them without debate. There are numerous examples of this process in every state in the Union. All an individual has to do is open his or her eyes and read past the politics.

Finally, I would just like to ask a simple question. Why do individuals who become elected officials always leave their position in a better financial situation than when they first started their term? I mean, I am not the smartest person in the world but I have never seen one of these individuals say, "I need to get back to my job of being an electrician, a beautician, or even a teacher." This is because our politicians of today are already bought and paid for before they even enter into office. The individuals that fund their campaign, the individuals that are in their camp are only concerned about their own personal goals and not about the education of our children. It seems to me that it is a real simple thing to fund the right amount of tax dollars to education. I am a big believer that the two most important individuals that our tax dollars should defiantly take care of are our children and our elderly. Our politicians feel these are the two groups that should suffer the most when there is a financial shortcoming. Wouldn't it be refreshing to see our politicians cut tax dollars to the many so-called pork recipients and give the money to better the education of our children? See, this will never happen with the individuals we have in office now because that very action threatens their wealth. Being elected to serve the people used to be an honorable unselfish job, now it is a career. The career has become one where the politician only dreams of wealth and power and not how he or she can make our educational system the best in the world. We truly need to find individuals who are knowledgeable and experienced in education. We need to find individuals who are unselfish and do not give in to the parasites who only want to use them to execute their selfish plans.

CHAPTER 2

NON EDUCATIONAL
ADMINISTRATORS, POLITICIANS,
AND THE MEDIA

I STARTED TEACHING IN 1979 at a very small high school in Sumter County. The school had four administrators: one principal, two assistant principals, and one dean. All of these individuals were 40 plus years of age and had spent at least ten or more years in the classroom. They were what I will call educational administrators because these individuals came into education wanting to be teachers and coaches. They had an excellent understanding of how the school functioned and the demographics of the student population. They were long-standing contributors of the community. They were well respected and personable. These individuals were part of a school as inexperienced first year teachers, following through to experienced classroom teachers and now to administrative positions that they had a vested interest in. Through their experience, these individuals had a good understanding of what students, teachers, and fellow administrators were going through in the school year. These individuals were able to make decisions based on sound educational experience and what was best for the school as a whole. It was a real positive experience for me because these individuals had the experience in the classroom to guide me as I struggled through my first year. It was reassuring for me to know that the administrator I was working for had already dealt with a lot of the problems I was facing and his advice was always right on target.

As I moved through the 1980s in my educational career, educational administrators were still the norm in the public school system. These were all individuals who started their educational careers as teachers and remained as teachers for ten plus years. As a consequence of their teaching for many years, these individuals gained valuable educational experience and knowledge about the organization, discipline, and management of the classroom environment. The educational administrators of the 1980s came from the classroom were they had experienced such things as overcrowding, lack of funding, discipline issues, and classroom management. They could relate to teachers and understand the issues teachers were facing year to year because they themselves had experienced the same or similar types of issues during their ten plus years of classroom management. They could relate to students because of the skills that were developed from all the different personalities they faced in their classroom teaching. The educational administrators of the 1980s did not distance themselves from the teachers or students because they always considered themselves classroom teachers first. The school came first and everything else took a back seat. The educational administrators looked at themselves as being an administrator at their perspective schools for the rest of their educational careers. These administrators wanted to plant their roots and grow with the school.

As the 1990s rolled in, there began to be a change in the philosophy of selecting school administrators and as a consequence the overall attitude of the administrators themselves began to have a negative change. The first was not allowing administrators to stay at a school for more than five years. I first begin to be aware of this when rumors would begin to circulate at the end of the school year about what principals were being transferred. I could never understand this type of thinking because I always thought if a school was functioning at a high level and the administrators had a good rapport with teachers, students, and the community then why change it. If administrators at a school are working well together and everyone associated with the school community is happy there should be no change. School districts of the 1990s and present day feel as though they have to change things even if they are wrong. I think because there is a lack of true educational experience at the district level there is confusion on what we are really trying to achieve academically. I think some district personnel feel threatened when a school administrator starts to gain support within his or her educational community. The noneducational administrators (NEAs) at the top have an attitude that they are more superior than anyone below them and when someone begins to gain too much success it is time to cut him or her down. These NEAs lack the knowledge and the experience to understand they are working with and not in competition with anyone below them. I mean, I do not know about you but why change something that is not broken? School districts and the media have developed this way of thinking and it is destroying our schools. Why not develop the philosophy of leaving administrators alone who are successful and finding better ones for low performing schools? Also why are we not looking at the successful administrators and seeing what and how they do things? We have professional development for teachers. Why not have professional development for potential school administrators? The problem here is our noneducational school district personnel do not get themselves out in the schools enough to know the qualities of a good, effective administrator. The school districts are only concerned with statistical test scores on a piece of paper and not what is really happening on a personal basis at the school. Why is it that all evaluations toward administrators are toward test scores and not their interaction with students, teachers, and the community?

I have a problem with superintendents in this day and age

too. Where are they and what exactly do they do all day? I have worked in my school district for a long time and I have yet to see our superintendents (we have a superintendent, deputy superintendents, area superintendents, and I am sure some other individuals with superintendent in their title that I do not know exist and that is the reason for the plural usage) at the school for a strictly educational visit. Oh yea, they have come to our school on some minor occasions, but these occasions were always politically motivated. It is a shame that individuals at the district level use their job as a stepping stone to political aspirations. Why do they not concentrate their efforts on helping the teachers and the educational administrators to help students? I have always wondered how superintendents could possibly understand the community of their schools when they make no effort to observe the day-to-day happenings at the school. In large school districts, a superintendent literally should have little time for politics if he or she is out observing schools. Here is what I am saying: These individuals are not true educators because a true educator would want to be where the educational process is taking place. A true superintendent of the schools would be in the schools on a day-to-day basis. A true superintendent when given a choice of visiting a school or going to some function related to political or personal gains would always choose the visitation to the school. This problem is not only with the superintendents but also with other district level personnel. If you are a teacher reading this book, I am sure you can relate to what I have just stated. We have noneducational individuals with limited or no educational experience making decisions at the district level and that absolutely amazes me. Take for example, one of the years I was mathematics department chair and the assistant principal over mathematics (who is what I would classify as an educational administrator) decided we needed a more applicable mathematics course for our students who are not college bound. The current course they were enrolled in was not meeting the academic and life skills the students needed for success in life. So the assistant principal called the district administrator in charge of mathematics and explained our situation. The response we received was typical of a noneducational administrator. The response from the county administrator was relayed to all math teachers in an e-mail from our school assistant principal. The e-mail described how we as a math department could select to use another math course that he recommended but as of then there was no textbook or set curriculum for the course from the county. He also informed us that the textbook for the course we are currently teaching will not be adopted for the next year and the course will be phased out. This is so typical of the type of choices being made at the district level. In this situation, they are expecting students to be enrolled in a course for which teachers have no textbook, no type of curriculum order, and no resource materials to help enhance the learning process. Teachers are expected to work through the development of the course while classes are in session. This would be like a doctor trying to perform an operation with no instruments and no type of operational order. If you think about it, this indicates that these students will get a fraction of the learning that they would normally acquire. It does not make sense when the district that is going to offer a course does not have all available materials to ensure the students have the greatest possible potential to learn and allow teachers to concentrate on how to teach the concept rather than knowing what concept is to be taught.

The next problem with today's administrators is how they get were they are. Individuals entering into education have found it easy to advance to an administrative position. Most of the requirements today to become an administrator deal with a higher level degree in some type of supervision or leadership, a certain number of years as a teacher, and some type of district requirement (this might be an internship, courses, or the experience of being a dean.). I know the requirement for being in the classroom in my district is three years. I am sure it is not much more in other school districts. This means, an individual can come into the educational profession and work in the classroom for one year, then become a dean for the remaining two years, and qualify (as long as he/she has a higher level degree in leadership) to go into the assistant principal pool. If you think about this, we are producing administrators that literally have no experience in the classroom. Thus these administrators have no educational experience. How are these individuals able to make sound decisions about educational issues within and about the school at which they are assigned? These NEAs have not dealt with discipline problems in the classroom or out in the halls. They have not dealt with looking out into a class full of students and reading faces to make sure all students understand the material you just presented. These NEAs have not had to deal with parental issues and the lack of parenting. They have not had to deal with beginning teachers and helping them cope with the overwhelming problems and issues they face. It is a very sad situation when an administrator who was a classroom teacher for only three years evaluates a teacher who has been teaching for fifteen plus years. There are methodologies that the experienced teacher has acquired through experience that the NEA cannot and will not ever understand. I can remember being evaluated (AP Statistics class) by an administrator and this particular individual I knew for a fact was in the actual classroom only for a year. After the evaluation, we met and the administrator gave me a few negative comments on the fact that my students were talking when they were working on problems and she felt it was not good for the learning environment. My response to the administrator was, "What were they talking about?" He or she responded the students were talking and discussing the problems. I looked at this individual and explained that in mathematics it is a very good thing when students are helping each other understand the problems. I believe in education we call it cooperative learning. I also told this administrator if this is the biggest thing I have to worry about, then my classes are in great shape. This administrator had seen the term cooperative learning in textbooks and in courses that he or she took but because of the lack of experience in the classroom did not have an idea of what cooperative learning looks like when implemented. Here is the point I hope that anyone reading this book will understand—individuals in education who have ten plus years in the classroom are not the bad guys. I know the media and our politicians have done a good job of influencing the public into thinking that anyone who has been in education for more than ten years is an incompetent, old-fashioned, lazy individual stealing money from the taxpayers. The fact is that these are the individuals we need to make good sound educational decisions—not decisions based on political or financial rewards. Educational experience can be gained only by classroom teaching and not by reading a book or listening to some lecture. It is the sound educational experience in the classroom that is lacking in today's educational system.

The lack of classroom experience with NEAs also creates issues with the enforcement of discipline. Up until about 1986, students knew that discipline issues would be dealt with administrators who had extensive experience in the classroom and already knew all the excuses and stories that could be told. The administrators of this time were educators and considered themselves equal to their teachers not above them. In the last twenty-five years, this way of thinking has shifted to NEAs believing they are above their teachers and their support in discipline matters has suffered because of a lack of educational experience. Today's NEAs have not spent day after day with students in the classroom to experience the culture of the student population. They have not encountered all the possible scenarios that develop with students through the course of every day. They have not had to make decisions as a teacher about certain educational situations whether right or wrong and learn from the consequences of those decisions. Finally the NEAs have not had year after year of these experiences to add to a bank of knowledge that would allow them to make informed educational decisions. Many of today's NEAs are gaining their educational experience while in their administrative duties. This results in careless half-thought decisions that could produce damaging consequences. There was a situation just about a year ago with a new NEA at our school. We had an assembly for the students the last two periods of the day. It was a talent show and through the course of the assembly it got pretty rowdy. A veteran teacher and I suggested to the administrator that we should end the show early because the buses were already there and allow the students to leave the gym one section at a time. His response was that the students were fine and they were having a lot of fun. We tried to explain to the administrator that there will be a safety issue with all the students leaving at the same time and he told us we could leave; so we did. The next day we heard that when the students left from the assembly there had been a lot of pushing and shoving that resulted in four different fights and about eleven students being suspended. I am sure the next time this administrator is in charge of an assembly he will make a more responsible decision. It is a shame that the administrator had to learn this at the expense of eleven students being suspended because it all could have been prevented.

There is also the problem of administrators from a certain discipline having to evaluate teachers from other disciplines. This has developed because all the standardized testing has changed the job description for a school administrator. In the last fifteen years, state politicians have placed so many requirements and so many changes in the curriculum in our public schools that the job of being an administrator is less and less dealing with the actual educational process in the classroom. Today's administrator is overwhelmed with all the statistics related to the test, all the special programs related to the test, and all the useless teacher development related to the test. It is all about the test. This test philosophy limits administrators in their actual interaction with teachers and students. For a true educator the choice is simple—stay in the classroom were I can truly do what I came into this profession to do. Because the educational teachers in mathematics, science, English, and the social sciences choose to stay in the classroom, this results in the pool of potential administrators coming from areas such as elementary and middle schools and again individuals with very little experience in the classroom. This creates the problem of administrators with a middle school English background evaluating science or mathematics teachers. I had a situation where an administrator with an elementary school background came in to evaluate me while I was teaching trigonometry to my class. I was involved so much in my teaching that I did not pay attention to the administrator in my classroom. The next day, my students came in to class and began to ask me who that individual was. I explained to them that it was one of the assistant principals who came to evaluate my teaching. I was shocked that some of the students did not even recognize one of their assistant principals. The real kicker was when one of my students made the comment—"I do not know how he or she evaluated you." I asked this student what he meant and quite a few of my students began to describe how the assistant principal had fallen asleep multiple times during the period. I am not trying to discredit any individual. I am only trying to make the point that if I were ask to evaluate an English teacher's class, I very well might fall asleep as well because I am not interested in English and I am in no way qualified to tell an English teacher what they are doing right let alone what they are doing wrong. From an administrative perspective, we have completely gone away from trying to improve teaching in the classroom.

And if we really want to look and see the lack of educational experience that is hidden, just look at the district level. There are so many makeshift titles invented for individuals who could not cut it not only in the classroom but also at the administrative level. I get e-mails all the time of some individuals and how they have now been promoted to be the assistant to the person in charge of interdisciplinary activities. I mean, come on what the hell are interdisciplinary activities anyway? Just like in business in today's world, education is very, very top heavy and nobody wants to point the finger in that direction. It always amazes me when politicians talk about budget cuts—the first thing always mentioned is about losing teachers. Let's see and do some math here: If a teacher on an average is making $40,000 a year and we have district administrators making $100,000 plus a year—Wow! I can save two-and-a-half teachers for every worthless administrative position in existence at the district level. This does not happen because the district is loaded with noneducational individuals and therefore they are not going to eliminate their own. To me it is like a fraternity at the district level and the fraternity protects their own. The media and politicians are quick to point the finger at the incompetent teachers. Why are they not quick to point the finger at the incompetence at the district level? I am also convinced that politicians have learned that if they want to get public attention, they then start mentioning about cutting teachers. Think about it if the media came out and said the state is making budget cuts and the state has decided to cut 25 politicians and 25 administrators at each educational district, the public would probably cheer and celebrate—I know I would (after I pick myself off the ground from shock). The fact is just like in state and federal governments where positions and salaries are hard to justify, educational districts have developed into their own little political entities. I have been to my district office and it is unbelievable to see the number of people who are walking around and doing nothing. I am not alone in this assessment. Teachers are held accountable for their actions during a whole teaching day. Why aren't administrators and other district personnel held accountable for their actions in a whole working day? I am not trying to portray all administrators and all district personnel as being incompetent. I am trying to make people aware that not only are there teachers who should not be in the classroom, there are also administrators and district personnel who have no business being in the positions they are in.

Lastly, I just want to mention the media and the roll it as played in the myth of our schools and how poorly they are performing. I do not understand how an individual who has never been in a public school classroom as a teacher can have such a strong opinion on education.

I really thought that a reporter's job was to report facts on both sides of the story and allow readers to form their own opinion. I am sure the journalistic procedure is to make sure that your statements are backed up by sound research. Here lies the problem because reporters today just want to make the paper and report anything that might cause controversy. We have such a reporter in my town. This reporter has produced numerous commentaries on education and I have to say that he is the most manipulative writer I have read. As an example, my district was looking into late start times for high schools and this switch to late start times was all financially motivated. This reporter wrote a commentary in support of the late start times and used for support a study that he thought gave evidence of the benefits for late start times. I went to the Web site and began to read the study and it had no support against or for the late start times. The study (a legitimate research study) used surveys as a basis of data. In fact, almost all of the so-called data was based on opinions. So I did some research and found numerous research studies stating exactly the same conclusions; there is no real statistical evidence one way or the other. I e-mailed this journalist and brought to his attention; he basically ignored what I sent and stated he did not have time to discuss it. My point is, there are a lot of journalists out there who think they are an authority on education just because they write about it. I am really tired of articles that depict issues in education in a biased way especially when they come from individuals who have no experience in the educational field.

Our politicians and some journalists have led the public into believing that education should be run like a business, and the state educational commissioner, the administrators who are in charge of the districts, and principals who run schools should perform their duties in a business way. The decisions they make should be based on good business and the saving of a few dollars. I am sorry to inform everyone that education is not a business, it is a gift. It is a gift that through the years has been given without greed and concern of financial involvement. Our forefathers saw how important it was to offer education to all American citizens. This was expanded through many years of debate and lobbying to include minorities. Up until the last few years, education was viewed as a gift that we as the citizens of the United States wish to allow our daughters and sons to have the opportunity to achieve. The decisions that are now being made with education are a direct neglect of these principles. We have allowed governmental officials to mislead the public into thinking our school districts and our schools need to be run like a business. Now think about this: When in this present day have you seen a business make decisions based on what is best for the employees who work for them and not based on a financial gain? And when they make these decisions do the owners, managers care how it affects the employees? I think not. This is what our politicians have turned our educational system into. There is no concern in their decisions for the students. They use a smokescreen to keep the students from being apart of the issues by presenting dollar figures that appear to be detrimental to the state as a whole. There is always the threat of increased taxes. There is the threat of the state going bankrupt, but there always seems to be enough money to cover some politicians' promises to their campaign contributors and lobbyists. As I stated before, education is a gift and it is a gift we are supposed to be giving to our children. So why aren't we making sure this gift is not the best we can possibly give? When are we ever going to hear from our politicians they have increased spending in education and have decreased spending in their own personal political agendas?

CHAPTER 3

ELIMINATING STUDENT CHOICE

FOR AS LONG AS THERE as been education in schools, I am pretty sure there have been two types of students. There are the students who aspire to go to college for whatever reasons and there are the students who know that college is not for them because of their interests in a trade or vocational area. Both sets of students are driven in their educational futures by a passion or curiosity in a field of interest. Both types of students are learning and absorbing knowledge in the particular subject area they pursue. The classes that both types of students are enrolled in are academic to each individual student in the class. In the 1970s and 1980s the schools were designed to accommodate both of these types of students. The schools curriculum gave both groups a general academic education in mathematics, science, English, and the social sciences. When the general academic education was complete, students were allowed to select electives in higher level academic subjects, vocational courses, the arts or all three. Students felt freedom in being able to investigate different academic areas of learning and in the process learn more about themselves. I would like the reader to understand that I believe any subject that involves learning should be considered academic. So vocational courses, courses in the arts and performing arts are academic courses that add to the development of the overall student. As a student in the 1970s and 1980s you were given the opportunity to take classes like woodshop, auto mechanics, child-development, business courses, home education courses, and courses in the arts. Every year of your high school education you were able to select one or more of these courses as electives and find if you had a talent for these areas. These elective courses gave students who were not college bound a reason for going to school and completing their education. These same elective courses allowed students who were college bound to gain knowledge of a skill or subject area that they normally might not be able to pursue. If you are an individual who is thirty-eight years of age or older, think of your education—it truly was a great time to be in school.

Today's students are held captive by the political decisions made by a select few who have no experience in education. Politicians for many years now have used the media to convince the public that our schools are failing our students. In the process, the politicians have used the evidence of lower test scores and sagging graduation rates to implement standardized testing in our schools. They have used studies such as Education Week's Quality Counts survey to let the public know where their state educational system stands in relation to other states' educational systems. The problem with these so-called studies is they are survey based and therefore opinion based. I have gone to the particular Web sites of these organizations and it is interesting that I could not find any link that allowed me to see the documents that were used in the evaluation process. I also looked to see the particular make up of the organization and found donors to be from places such as Met-Life, Bill Gates, Hewlett, and the Joyce Foundation to name a few. I am not an expert on any of these donors but I do know that some of them do have political affiliations. Are the political connections within these organizations a cause for concern with the validity of the data that has resulted with these educational studies? Do these organizations have a significant influence on the studies? Is there some type of agenda these organizations wish to support through their donations? Here is the problem, how do you really compare one state's educational system to another state's educational system. The point I am trying to have you as the reader think about is when comparing one state's educational system to another state's educational system there are a lot of variables that play into the statistics. The educational needs of the students in Florida are not the same educational needs as the students in Tennessee because demographics, size, culture, and most importantly, the political decisions made. These types of studies provide weak evidence of a state's standing in the country as far as education. Unfortunately, the producers of such worthless studies know that the general public does not take the time to investigate the validity of the study. First of all, how can you compare one state's state test to another state's state test when they are not the same instrument? How can you look at the graduation rate of states like Texas, Florida, New York, and California to states in the mid-west. Texas, Florida, New York, and California are all transient states, meaning these states have a heavy flow of students who are in their schools one day and gone the next day. Organizations like Education Weekly know the public will only be concerned with the ranking their particular state receives in relation to the other states, not in the statistics used to produce the results. Sure, the general education that all students should have is basically the same but there are a lot of variables to consider when looking at the individual states and not all states have the exact same set of variables. These types of studies influence our political leaders to fund money in places of little value to our students' overall education. In Florida, we have numerous organizations, activities, and programs that have been cut or eliminated because our politicians do not even understand the real validity of these surveys. The politicians fund money to areas that help boost the statistical state values on these worthless surveys and make our state look better superficially. In the mean time, our students are being exposed to a less creative individual educational experience. If we are concerned with our students developing as a whole, should they not have the opportunity to learn vocational skills, learn the arts, or learn some other specialized skills not related to the core courses? States with standardized testing have strategically taken this privilege away from their students.

Students in states where standardized testing is used for accountability have been separated from their ability to choose courses outside the core curriculum and enhance their creative skills. These students are given the mandates that increase the number of years they have to take their core courses. An example is in Florida where students are now required to take four years of mathematics as opposed to three years. Politicians have sold the public on the idea that students need this extra year in mathematics in order to be successful in later life. This extra requirement in mathematics results in students having one less spot in their schedule to take an elective course. Now you may be thinking it is not a bad thing and it is only one elective they cannot take. Here lies the problem. First of all, it is a requirement for all students and if you think about it, the students who are "college material" are going to use their elective to take an extra mathematics course anyway. It hurts the students who are not "college material" because these students would use their elective to take a course that interests them and might possibly help them to understand what they would like to do the rest of their lives. This in turn reduces the enrollment of these elective courses and NEAs now eliminate these courses from the schedule. This is what has happened in Florida. Since the arrival of the FCAT, I have seen (within the district) the elimination of courses such as auto mechanics, drafting, child-development, and multiple business courses just to name a few. The kicker is that there were students who wanted these courses and the equipment was already in place and because of standardized testing issues these students were not allowed to experience the learning involved in these classes. As an example, our school had just purchased eleven driving simulators around the year of 2002 for our drivers' education classes. These are very expensive machines and they are used to simulate driving conditions without having to use a real car. A year later, when the state mandated more remedial classes for Florida's students who did not score well on the state test, drivers' education was eliminated from the curriculum and the simulators were sold for a fraction of the cost to some outside source. I just do not understand how we eliminate such programs when the demand exists and the equipment is bought and paid for. Can you explain it to me? I have tried to make sense of why our politicians make such regulatory decisions with education and the only reason I see is control. If the politicians control what our students are learning, then they basically control the whole country without debate. Do you see our politicians regulating big business or big corporations? No, these organizations want the freedom and creativity to expand their progress. Why do we not have the same philosophy with our educational systems? Let our students have the freedom and the creativity to progress in a way that they have a choice.

As mentioned earlier, another negative affect that has developed with standardized testing and the state-to-state comparative studies is if you are a student who does not pass the state standardized test, the state has required the student to take remedial courses in the areas where the student performed poorly. This means if a student does not pass both mathematics and verbal portions of the test, he or she is required to take a remedial mathematics course and a remedial reading course. If these two courses are added to the regular schedule of mathematics, English, science, and a social science there is no room for a student to take an elective. What needs to be understood is that this student will continue to take the remedial courses for as long as he or she does not score high enough on the test to allow them pass. Literally, a student can come in as freshman and never take an elective for his or her entire high school career because of remediation classes. I ask you, is this fair to students who know from the very beginning they are not college bound. The group of students who are not college bound deserve to have the opportunity to explore different elective courses to help them in understanding more about themselves. All students need to have the freedom of selecting their own electives. All students should have the right to have a decision in the education they receive. Students do not need the score on a one-day test to determine what they should be taking the next year. I can understand why there is such a problem with students and their lack of enthusiasm with their education. It is hard for students to get excited about their education when they have very little input on the decisions. It is the student's education not the state or federal governments. It is the student and his or her family that has the right and the freedom to have available more elective courses and the right to select from them on the schedule and not the government.

The elective courses outside the core courses are important in the fact that they allow students to become creative and invent new ideas and if we eliminate them from the curriculum we take our students abilities to be creative. These types of courses help students to find out about themselves in a different perspective. The core courses teach students about facts and knowledge related to already discovered concepts, terms, or skills. These courses give a background and a foundation for creativeness later in life. The elective courses such as art, woodshop, drafting, etc., give students skills that they expand on and use in their own creative way. These elective courses allow students to think outside the general rules or guidelines of the skill. The elective courses show students how to express themselves and determine the more personal qualities about themselves. Since standardized testing has been enforced, the school systems have forgotten how important this is in the overall growth of the student. I am currently teaching AP statistics and one day I decided to get a feel for what current students were thinking in terms of elective courses. The first question I asked was, "Did you know that courses such as drafting, auto mechanics, child development, and multiple business courses used to be offered at this school?" I was shocked that well over half my students in five statistics classes did not even know these classes were once part of the curriculum. This is sad and we have allowed it to happen. I then ask my students that if these classes were offered today how many of them would take one or more of them. The response was hundred percent. Every student in my five classes said they would take at least one of the elective classes. I am convinced that politicians do not want our students to be creative. Politicians have used standardized testing to standardize our students. Standardization in education means everyone thinks the same. When dealing with problems, every student is taught the same steps in order to solve. Every teacher is to use the same methodologies when instructing his or her students. If you really think about this, it is an easy way to make society easy to govern. I wonder if our politicians want to purposely take away the creative thinking of our students—to standardize our students so that they are dependent upon the government and the politicians. I hear complaints all the time about how these kids today cannot think for themselves, and what everyone needs to understand is that this is a result of standardized testing. Standardized testing in our educational system means control and this is exactly what our politicians want.

Now let's talk about how standardized testing has influenced Advance Placement courses. The College Board began running the Advanced Placement program since 1955 and the original goal of these courses was to allow students to take a college-level course and possibly get college credit for the course. These AP courses were taught at the college level and the students enrolled in the classes were probably in the upper 20 percent of the schools population. Completion of the course did not constitute receiving college credit. A student would have to score a 3 or higher on a five-point scale in an end-of-year exam in order to be considered for college credit. Because the courses are demanding, students involved in any particular Advanced Placement class need to be self-disciplined and focused on their study skills. These students need to be creative in their problem-solving skills. I cannot speak for other states but the state in which I teach has made the AP courses a part of the grading system for school scores. The problem is that the scoring is based on the number of students enrolled in AP classes and not whether the students score high enough on the AP test. Sure the state is awarding bonus points on a school's passing rate on AP exams but the fact that they are only bonus points does not make it as attractive to work for as enrolling as many students as possible in AP courses. This has caused all high schools to enroll as many students as possible into some AP class in order to receive the points for the school grade. The open enrollment of AP courses creates two problems. First, there is the understanding that in prerequisite courses, the students are only learning how to pass the standardized test. This means, students are drilled in generic learning strategies that are specifically geared toward passing the standardized test. Students are not learning higher-level problem-solving skills and as a result, struggle in AP courses. These students usually come in to these AP courses and either drop after a certain time period or make an average or below-average grade in the course. Second, because there are more students struggling with the AP course, teachers are adapting the course in such a way as to help these students be successful. I guess the phrase "watering down" is appropriate here. The level of expectation is lowered because teachers are feeling the pressure about failure rates. Please understand that the blame for any type of "watering down" of a course is not with the teacher or the student. It is a situation that has been created through the lack of educational experience and standardized testing development. I hate to keep emphasizing the same point but the changes that AP classes are experiencing in my state are a direct result of the standardized testing issue. Politicians do not concern themselves with AP courses being adjusted to accommodate the standardized student because the politicians really do not care about the educational process. There was nothing wrong with the way AP classes were being taught. Politicians have again used these courses to invoke change for political reasons.

There is a very high percentage of politicians who have no experience in education and as a result, when they make decisions for education, the decisions are usually costly to the taxpayers, the students, and the teachers. Most of the politicians never voice an opinion about educational issues, they just vote. Most of them probably have not even read the bill, they just vote. Is there something very wrong about this? Did we not elect these individuals to have a genuine concern for the issues? I believe that politicians look at the people in their perspective areas as individuals who are well below them socially. Politicians have an attitude that taxpayers, students, and teachers cannot and will not ever challenge their decisions because we are not bright enough to see through them. Politicians have placed themselves in the upper level of the food chain. To me, politicians have focused on one thought, "How can I make the public think I really care about education in order to get or stay elected?" In my years as an educator, I have not seen a single politician who really showed some concern about the education of our children. Sure, there are a lot who talk a good game but not one have I seen make education a priority in their political career.

Taxpayers and teachers have no excuses for not holding their politicians accountable for the decisions they make for education. We can exercise our voting rights and elect them out of office. It is a really alarming to see that very few teachers, police officers, or firemen ever get elected to political office. There is such a misrepresentation of careers in our political positions. The really sad thing is nobody has bothered to speak up for the students. The curriculum in our high schools has been overhauled to the point where it is a mere fraction of what used to be available for students to have the opportunity to learn. It is really sad to me when I ask students if they miss courses such as drafting, business, and other eliminated courses and they respond with bewilderment because they have no idea what the courses are or what the course could have taught them. I am sorry but I have always believed that the United States of America was always about freedom and the ability to have choices. Today's politicians have forgotten this in the educational curriculum and continue to dismantle an educational system that is not only the best in the world but the most effective in the world.

CHAPTER 4

TRYING TO ELIMINATE TEACHERS WITH MULTIPLE EXPERIENCE

ANOTHER MISCONCEPTION THAT HAS BEEN used by politicians as they attempt to dismantle public education is their accusations involving the inability of older teachers to perform in the classroom. Politicians want the public to believe that teachers who have been teaching for over twenty years are in service only because they have to buy time until retirement. The truth to the matter is that individuals who have been teaching for over twenty years are still in service because they continue to enjoy teaching. Politicians fail to acknowledge the vast number of experienced teachers who are the foundation of any good school. They have convinced the public that individuals out of the field of education would make better teachers in the classroom. Politicians base this view not understanding that teaching is an art and it is developed through a desire to be in the classroom and work through all the obstacles that present themselves on a day-to-day basis. They say teachers need some type of merit pay and need to get away from the current pay based on experience so that the nonproductive teachers can be identified. Politicians have used the same statistics such as graduation rates and falling test scores to convince the public that experienced educationally degreed teachers are at the heart of these problems. Politicians argue that the older teachers are stuck in the ways that they teach and are not open to new ideas. They claim older teachers are not either willing or capable of using technology in the classroom. Politicians and the media use the fact that teachers have a retirement fund and are able to use this fund to double dip to create a negative attitude that teachers are receiving more than they deserve. Politicians and the media continue year after year to blame teachers for the difficulties in public education and year after year the government continues to reduce spending in public education.

The idea that anyone can teach in our educational system is not only wrong, it gives the perception that individuals who do come from college educational programs are ineffective tools in the classroom. Politicians have expressed this in many ways. They have issued initiatives that have given bonus monies to individuals coming out of the workforce to teach in the classroom. They have offered to scrap off college loans for individuals majoring in mathematics or science if they will come into the classroom. I can tell you from my experience as head of the mathematics department in the last ten years, we have had eleven individuals come from the outside world and think they wanted to teach; only one of them stayed with it and is still teaching today. These individuals that come from the workforce realize real quick how difficult it is to teach today. Nothing irritates me more than hearing some individual say something to the effect of "I can always teach." This gives the impression that teaching requires no skill, no training, and no professionalism. Let's clear some things up right now. First, teaching requires so much skill that it is impossible to ever be completely or totally skilled in the art of teaching. Teachers have to be skilled in the art of evaluation. Teachers have to be able to stand in front of one classroom at a time and be able to evaluate the class as a whole and each individual student. It takes a lot of experience to be able to look out at the class full of students and be able to read their faces and their actions as to whether they understand what you have just presented. A teacher has to be able to walk through the halls and evaluate every single student and the potential for issues that need to be resolved before there are serious consequences. This type of evaluation skill is only acquired through years of experience and not by someone who has only worked in the profession for a couple of years. Teachers have to possess the skill of adaption. In the last few years, teachers have had to adapt to so many changes that our politicians with no educational experience have put forth. And the teachers who have adapted to these changes are not those with a few years of experience because a good majority of them have left the profession whether by choice or by budget cuts. It is the experienced teachers who have made the most of a very poor, selfish situation. I know that there are some experienced teachers who have no business to be in the classroom, but those types of teachers are a very small minority. Why do politicians and the media concentrate their efforts on this small minority and not put their efforts toward helping all of the good teachers? If you walk around any school in this country there is a high percentage of good teachers and very low percentage of bad teachers. We never seem to want to report, "Hey, fifty four out of the sixty teachers we have in our school are good and excellent teachers." I wonder if politicians would start promoting all the effective teachers and wouldn't force some of the bad teachers to step it up.

As I write this book, the hot topic that is still alive and always will be is the idea of merit pay for teachers. Politicians have again convinced the public that the way teachers are paid is a waste of taxpayer dollars because it allows the incompetent teachers to be paid just as equally as the competent teachers. Politicians have somehow (and I am not sure how they have done it) transformed the merit pay issue into an attack on experienced teachers. The media has written articles that support teachers with less experience receiving the same or more amount of pay than more experienced teachers. The argument they make is that there are teachers with less experience who perform better in the classroom than some of the more experienced teachers. I understand this and I do not disagree. I would like you to understand the comparison is always made between a less-experienced teacher and a teacher with bad experience. Politicians never seem to want to promote the experienced teachers who year after year continue to produce strong students from their classrooms. My problem in this evaluation process is how politicians are going to determine who is performing well and who is not. I know that the big push is through standardized testing and performance on these tests. Some states are going to use the state test as a determining factor. Other states are going to use end-of-the-course exams. Regardless of what is used, the bottom line is that politicians know that it is a topic that the public would like to see implemented, but they do not have a clue as to how to achieve such an evaluation tool. The reason it is such a hard thing to do is that there are so many other variables that go into the making of an effective teacher. How do you measure the ability a teacher has to motivate his or her students? How do you measure the ability a teacher has to enhance creative thinking skills of the students? How do you measure a teacher's ability to give students the ability to improve themselves? How do you measure a teacher's ability to teach a student to be a well-rounded, contributing member of our society? And there are many, many more qualities that go into being a competent teacher. I know some of the individuals who have no experience in education will argue that a standardized test will represent these qualities. My question is "How?" I know of some teachers out there and their student's test scores would probably give them an average grade as a teacher. But the reality is that they are the very best at what they do because they teach more than test-taking skills; they teach how to be successful. These teachers work with their students at all levels of their educational development. These are experienced teachers who know one of the most important things we can teach these students is how to pick themselves up and keep going after they have been knocked down. There are experienced teachers who are masters at motivating students into being able to achieve more than what the student really thought he or she could achieve. Experienced teachers help students change their negative undisciplined qualities into positive self-disciplined characteristics. I wish there was a way to measure teachers and be hundred percent sure on their abilities to be competent teachers; unfortunately, there is no such way. We cannot use a single test to evaluate a teacher; the test has to be teamed up with actual qualitative observations to see exactly what is happening in the classroom. Merit pay is a difficult concept and the reason that it is such a very difficult thing to design a way to evaluate our teachers is the simple fact that teaching is a lot more complex and involved than we give the profession credit for.

I know that in my district, they have come up with a merit pay plan and it involves test scores and a complex observational process that has very little to do with actual methodologies in teaching. Here is the plan in a condensed form and you tell me if it makes sense. In the state of Florida, we are moving away from one standardized test and going to the method of having end-of-year exams. This is a good concept and I agree with end-of-year exams. The problem is, our politicians have insisted on end-of-year exams for what they call core courses. You see, the people of Florida passed a class size law and limited the core courses to not more than twenty-five students. At the time the law was passed, all mathematics, science, English, and social science courses were considered core courses. This cost the politicians a lot of money in the budget because a lot of teachers had to be hired to abide by the law. I guess the politicians received a lot of heat from their donors and their special interest groups because two years later they decided to reclassify mathematics courses such as calculus, statistics, precalculus, and science courses such as chemistry and physics as not being core. There are a lot of courses in other disciplines that received the reclassification but I will leave it to the readers to research this on their own. The reason I make this point is because the teachers who teach the now labeled noncore courses such as calculus, chemistry, precalculus, just to name a few, are going to be evaluated on the results of the end-of-year exams from the core courses such as algebra I and biology. I teach statistics and precalculus and my evaluation is not on the performance of the students I teach but on students in algebra I classes and students in geometry classes with whom I have no contact. Sounds like a good way to see if I am teaching my statistics students the right stuff. I mean seriously, can you see how absurd this is? I can have (hypothetically speaking) all my AP statistics students pass their AP test and if the algebra I students at my school do not score high enough, I get a poor evaluation. Not to mention the fact that just like it always plays out all the money and the resources will go to the students in the core courses because the people in administration could potentially lose their job if the students perform poorly. The evaluation process also involves administrators coming in the classroom and observing for certain criteria that is an insult to the art of teaching. I will not spend a whole lot of time on this aspect of the evaluation because the only thing that needs to be stated is there will be lot of nonacademic administrators performing evaluations in subject areas in which they are not trained or educated. I believe I have given a much more detailed discussion of this problem in another chapter.

Another accusation directed toward experienced teachers is their inability to change. Politicians have accused experienced teachers of being set in their ways of instructing students and not being open to new methodologies. Politicians want the public to believe that there are all these new technological tools that can be used in the classroom. The problem with this is that the politicians forget to budget the money to allow all teachers the ability to work with some or all these technological tools. Politicians want the public to believe that it is the older experienced teachers who will not change or adapt to new ways when in reality it is their lack of budgeting money to the right places that is the reason to this problem. I can honestly tell you if the technology is there for the teachers to use, it will get used by all of them. Politicians want the public to see experienced teachers as being outdated and needing to be put on the shelves. The truth of the matter is that these new methods that the states are pushing are really old methods that have been adapted for standardized testing. Experienced teachers are aware of this and continue to teach with their old methods because they really are all the same thing. I can only tell you that I have sat in many so-called professional development meetings only to realize that it was the same material I have seen countless times in my educational career. The presenters of these staff development seminars seem to be individuals who have lost touch with what is going on in the classroom. It looks to me as though some of these people present staff development to justify a job. There are so many of these useless meetings that I quit going to them. This is not a rebellion against meetings; it is a rebellion against pointless meetings, which have no impact on a student's learning. There are a few things to think about when trying to understand were I am coming from. These meetings take up valuable time that a teacher could spend tutoring students, working on lessons for the next class periods, or performing assessments on their students. I once sat in a meeting that was supposed to help teachers design higher order questions. The meeting was presented by an individual who had been in the classroom less than five years. The meeting was a waste of time because the presenter talked about the same sociological concepts (Blooms Taxonomy,) that I have heard for all thirty of my years as a teacher. There were twenty-one teachers at the meeting all with ten years or more experience and we all looked at each other like we have better things to do. The real tragedy was I had to tell three students who needed tutoring that I could not meet with them because of the meeting. I really feel that this whole multiple meeting concept has developed through the idea of running education like a business. In business, there are meetings to find ways to improve performance based on profits. Education's profits are a young person's mind and how it develops intellectually, spiritually, and emotionally. You gain more profits from a young person's mind from face-to-face interaction and not by keeping the teacher committed to countless meetings.

Something that has really had a negative impact on experienced, older teachers is the complaint politicians and the media are making on their retirement packages. These naysayers accuse experienced teachers of placing a huge financial burden on the state and its taxpayers and think the whole retirement formula needs to be restructured. I think there needs to be a clear understanding of the mathematics involved and I will explain the retirement system in my state of Florida as an example. Once I have finished, I think my points will relate to any state regardless of how the formula for their teacher's retirement is set up. As a teacher in Florida, if you teach for thirty years, your annual benefit is calculated by multiplying 48 percent times the average of your best five years. Police Officer and firefighters retirement is calculated by multiplying the years of experience by 3 percent. Police officers and firefighters can retire after twenty-five years; this gives them 75 percent of the average of their best five years. Public employees, which include our politicians, fall under the same mathematics except they would get 3.3 percent times the average of their best five years. Based on this math, teachers receive the lowest compensation for their pension and make the lowest salary. Here are a few points to be considered. The first point I would like to present is the simple known fact that teachers receive modest salaries for the work they perform and in tough financial times, teachers will not receive any type of raise at all. As a matter of fact, at the time that I am writing this book, many school districts have not given their teachers a real raise in over three years. And if you think about the way the economy has been, there is not an item essential for living in this world that has not increased in cost. My point is, teachers keep on teaching even through these unfortunate times because the retirement package is a positive they look forward to. The retirement benefit is based on a certain percent of a teacher's salary, each paycheck, and this is accumulated through the years.

The incentive is to stay in the profession long enough to collect this money in a monthly benefit to be able to survive when old age has taken its toll. The public needs to understand that this money is part of the whole salary package for a teacher. If teachers were given big enormous salaries like some professions, then there would be no need for a pension. This is not the case and the pension is an incentive to stay in teaching. My second point is politicians and the media have attacked these pensions saying they cost the state too much money, but they do not emphasize the point of all the senseless use of taxpayer dollars on pork bellies. I have never understood how whenever there is an economic meltdown, the media does not research and find all the ridiculous money that is given to organizations or projects that have no business being funded with taxpayer dollars. Instead, the media along with our bought-off politicians would rather take money from our teachers, police officers, and firemen retirement funds than not fund some type of project that only benefits a few. I can only imagine how many taxpayer dollars are wasted on favors but our politicians want to take away from our teachers. It does not make sense to me. The third point I would like to make is, I hear all the time how teachers are underpaid and underappreciated, but yet the attacks still persist on their retirement. It is funny how these thoughts seem to be eliminated from our politicians and the media in tight times. When is there ever going to be a politician who stands up and says I am not going to allow our schools to be a victim and does something about it? If there is one thing that a teacher does have to be proud of, it is the simple idea that if they work hard in the profession for many years they themselves and their families will be taken care of at an older nonworking age.

Along with this attack on teachers retirement within my state (and any other states that have a similar program) is the idea of the DROP program and the double dipping that takes place. First, I do not deny that the double dipping takes place. DROP stands for Deferred Retirement Option Program. It is a program where teachers can enter into the program after retirement and the selling point is they can continue to work up to eight years with retirement benefits going into a special trust that earns about 6.5 percent annual interest. When teachers enter into DROP they are required to delay their retirement benefits for as long as they stay in the program. Now let's think about this; the state tells the teacher—we are going to give you 6.5 percent interest on your retirement benefits in a special trust fund and meanwhile we are going to keep all your retirement fund that you have accumulated in the last thirty years and collect interest on it. I am not real sure but I think the interest collected by the state on the total retirement of a teacher is more than the 6.5 percent interest they are giving in the DROP. This means the state is making money on all teachers who enter DROP. So if the media would like to call this double dipping then so be it, but there is really very little extra cost being borne by the state. The real travesty is at the district level, the salaries are much larger and the potential of lump-sum money is quite large. It is a point of note that whenever the media reports abuse of the DROP program it is always with district administrators and not with teachers. Yet the media always seems to connect teachers to these district administrators even though the teachers' salaries are considerably less than the district administrators. I am sorry, but this is another example of our politicians and our media using teachers and programs associated with teachers to give inaccurate information in order to influence the public in a negative way toward true experienced educators and the job they perform.

Before I finish with this chapter, I would like to reemphasize the point of all the senseless spending that is performed by politicians who owe favors. A point to be made here is, look at all the millions of dollars that are raised for election campaigns. A couple of things that have always bothered me is, first, why is there no accountability for these funds. Why aren't politicians required to show where they got their funds from and how much? Why aren't politicians required to show their expenditures and if there is money left over where is it going to? In education, politicians want to wave a red flag for the spending associated with teachers. Why are they themselves not being considered? Second, why hasn't any media organization kept a watchful eye on where our tax dollars are going? I have seen dollars spent on athletic facilities, rail systems that the public voted against, and numerous other monies budgeted to items that had little positive effect on the population as a whole. Yet the media is in bed with the politicians when it comes to not allowing the public to be informed on what and how our tax dollars are being spent. I would really like to know how much the tax breaks are for certain companies and organizations. I would really like to see a comparative financial statement based on the money spent for retirement on our public service employees versus the money spent elsewhere in the state. I would also like to see the retirement for each individual government job be broken down for comparison purposes. It would be interesting to see what the mathematics tells us.

CHAPTER 5

EXTRACURRICULAR ACTIVITIES AND THEIR EDUCATIONAL EXPERIENCE

EXTRACURRICULAR ACTIVITIES INCLUDE ALL ATHLETIC programs, any type of club, band, cheerleading, drama, and leadership classes. These types of activities are still being offered at the high school level, but I have seen times where the politicians and district personnel have tried to (sometimes succeeding) restrict the overall structure of these activities. Anytime there have been financial hardships within the government or the district, politicians or district administrators always look for areas within the schools to save money. Through the years, extracurricular activities have always been hit in some shape or form. Unfortunately, when our so-called community leaders make their decisions on what and how much to cut, they do not figure into these decisions the long-term effects. The decisions to cut certain extracurricular activities have produced a financial hardship on parents to a point where their son or daughter is unable to participate. Through the years, I have seen our politicians or district administrators change the junior high system into a middle school system that has destroyed athletics and the maturity growth of our twelve to fifteen year olds. I have seen these same individuals eliminate certain junior varsity programs at the high school level and minimize the amount of participants in an individual sport or activity. These politicians and district administrators have restructured the practice start times and the schedules themselves so there is a question about safety and whether coaches are having the time to actually teach the fundamentals of their particular sport. Let me make it clear—our politicians and our district administrators have made decisions not based on sound educational experience but on easy, biased, financial quick-fix ideas.

I can remember twenty or so years ago there were elementary schools, junior high schools, and high schools. In the process of a student advancing his or her education, the student would go through six years of elementary school, three years of junior high school, and three years of high school. In each of the three steps, the student would start at a beginning not only in academic terms but also in extracurricular terms and advance to the top level. This means a student in first grade always looked forward to advancing five more years to become a sixth grader and being at the leadership position in the school. When graduating from elementary school the student would arrive at junior high school and again become the rookie in the school only to look forward to completing the next two years to again become the leader of his or her school. Once graduating from junior high school, the student would enter high school with the process being repeated with the final leadership position being taken as a senior in high school. With this process we have allowed our students to experience a maturity process three separate times in their academic careers that is invaluable to their overall growth as a human being. Not only would they experience this in academics but also through extracurricular activities. As an elementary student, I can remember waiting with great anticipation as I went through my grade school levels and was able to participate in different levels of extracurricular activities. In music, I can remember going from singing to learning how to play a little instrument called the Tonette to learning how to play the piano. In athletics, all the elementary schools had their own basketball teams with a junior varsity and a varsity. Junior varsity teams were made up of fourth and fifth graders and the varsity was made up of sixth graders. Most of the elementary activities were sponsored by an outside organization such as Boys or Girls club or the YMCA. Other extracurricular activities were offered through the elementary school and these outside organizations and the process was still working your way up to the leadership position. They were all programs generally funded by the state and were of little expense to the parents. The programs gave a lot of elementary aged students a chance to be a part of a team. It allowed these students to learn how to set goals for themselves and work for goals with other members of the team. It was a good beginning for a child beginning to learn self-discipline and gain higher self-esteem.

Leaving elementary school and going to junior high school brought about more opportunities to participate in extracurricular activities. These extracurricular activities were all sponsored and funded by the state and the district. There were school-sponsored athletic activities such as basketball, football, baseball, track, and soccer just to name a few. There were schools that sponsored performing arts programs such as chorus, band, theater, and various art clubs. There were school-sponsored extracurricular activities such Future Farmers, a woodworkers club, and what would be considered a quiz bowl team of academics. Teachers were provided supplements for sponsoring and coaching students in these activities. The coaching and leadership in these programs were of an extremely high quality because of the competition between other junior high schools in the area and the chance for advancement by the coaches and sponsors to the high school level. Students in junior high were able to experience the ideas of developing individual goals as well as team goals. This idea of working with the team to achieve team goals was a very important at this young age so the students could understand how to handle adversity without engaging in any form of violence. This was a great age for students to learn that there is consequence for every action and not all consequences are of a good nature. Junior high school was a place to teach students the beginning qualities of being a young adult.

Because junior high school included seventh through ninth grade, students again had to start as the rookies and work and learn to be the veterans of the school. Extracurricular activities helped students to advance through the phases of junior high. Extracurricular activities allowed these younger individuals to be a part of something that is supervised by an educated adult—a teacher/coach/sponsor who had a passion for the activities they are in charge of and transformed that passion to their students. These were individuals looking to ensure their players or participants understood the rules of the organization and that they were followed and abided by. They had discipline and knew they were supported in their disciplinary practices by the administration and the parents. Students at the middle school/junior high ages are very impressionable and it was the state and the school districts job to make sure that impression was a positive, morale one. Because of competitive sports, clubs that performed activities after school, and performing arts organizations' students were allowed to learn personal characteristics such as setting goals, self-discipline, and social skills that allowed them to work with a group for a common goal at a younger age. This was a valuable tool in keeping these younger students focused on fitness and positive morale decision-making skills. Junior high was the start of activities being solely associated with the school. Being a member of the schools athletic teams or the schools band, chorus, or any other school organization allowed these young adults to begin a positive developmental process that would carry into high school. The extracurricular activities made the academics side of school more acceptable to a group of students who otherwise would have been a problem. The extracurricular activities at this young age gave parents better control of their children.

Graduating from junior high gave students a solid foundation in discipline, maturity, and ability to succeed in the high school environment. Upon entering high school, the junior high graduates would already have some idea of the extracurricular activities they would like to pursue and would also be expose to more choices for extracurricular activities. Again the students would enter and be at the beginner's level of the high school social standing. These students would have many opportunities to observe and learn how to grow and develop into contributing adults in our society. At the high school level, there are three times as many clubs, athletic organizations, and extracurricular activities like band, drama, and chorus a student can become involved in. High school should become a stepping stone in a student's life helping them to understand where they are and where they are headed. Students came in contact with teachers, sponsors, and coaches who were instrumental in helping them find their likes and dislikes. Students at the high school level had the freedom of choice to choose what they wanted to learn and what they wished to participate in. This freedom of choice made high school an acceptable event in a lot of student's lives. If you think back to when you were in high school there may have been things that you did not appreciate but the one that you did have was the freedom of choice. The 1960s, 1970s, 1980s, and the very early years of the 1990s were times when the public school systems offered students and the teachers the freedom of choice. They were times when individual creative talents were not held down by mandates and requirements to satisfy the passing of a single standardized test.

Today's schools are far from the experience mentioned earlier. At the elementary level, young students are now stressed on their abilities to pass a standardized test and the promotion to another grade. They sit in classrooms were the lessons are geared toward passing the test. The teachers in the classroom are restricted in their creativity because of demands placed on them to use specific methodologies related to the standardized test. There are individuals who have no background in education sitting in their offices far away from the schools making decisions about what to teach, how to teach, and when to teach. Funds have been cut or rerouted to areas of a noncreative influence. By this I mean funds are rerouted from an art or music activity to buy more workbooks related to the standardized test. Students at the elementary level are being bombarded with lessons geared strictly with standardized test issues and not creative fun learning that students in this age group should be experiencing. Because of the lack of creative instruction and creative activities, these students are developing a sense of school being more like a job rather than a wonderful experience of discovery. Students at the elementary level are not having the chance to develop their own creative intelligence because of the standardization of instruction. Teachers at the elementary level are being held down from using their creative talents and making the classroom an enjoyable experience. Through standardized tests we are developing our elementary aged students into being good little followers and not good little leaders. The politicians are demanding this type of instruction in the classroom because it will produce the type of individual that makes it easy for them to rule. The extracurricular activities that were once associated with the elementary school have all been eliminated to make room for all the mandates from the politicians and the standardized testing demands. If you look at the poor health that are younger children are now in, all you have to do is understand how standardized testing has affected the elementary schools financially, in the lack of physical health curriculum, and the way administrators now think. It truly is not a fun time to be an elementary student and why parents are not recognizing this is in another chapter.

At the junior high or middle school level, politicians have cut budgets so drastically that there is only a shadow of what was once a strong extracurricular program. At this level, district personnel analyzed the financial situation and made decisions that eliminated or downsized specific programs in sports, performing arts, and clubs.

I am not quite sure why this was a solution because my understanding is that tax dollars are supposed to go to the overall education of our students. Even the programs that were saved were no longer completely funded by the district. These programs were extensively looked at and decisions were made on how to save money through equipment reduction, limited schedule, or pay to play. I am sorry but there is no way that any student or parent should have to pay to play in our public school system. This is where we have let our politicians gain the ability to not report to us were our tax dollars actually are going. It is a crying shame our politicians are not required to get approval from the public on expenditures in the private sector. The clubs and programs that were once associated with a uniform in school colors are no longer available. The programs that now exist have a PE t-shirt for a uniform, they meet or practice half the time they used to, and the schedule to compete or participate against other schools has been drastically reduced or altogether eliminated. There are not enough extracurricular activities available for all students to have a chance to participate, so they go home and play video games lying on the couch or join another team called a gang. The decrease in programs has caused the formation of an overwhelming amount of organizations that charge for participation in their program. Now parents have to spend hundreds of dollars for their son or daughter to be able to participate in an extracurricular activity. In the past, this was offered by the school district and was free. Why is it that we pay taxes to the government and those taxes do not go to support the well-being of our children? Most parents have to spend their post tax dollars to ensure their children are able to participate in some type of extracurricular activity. Junior high/middle schools are now institutions for learning in standardized, noncreative environments. I really feel for our students of today because they have to go through eight to nine years of being taught that the most important thing in their young academic lives is to pass a standardized test. The politicians have used the media to convince the public that this is the best education we can give our children. What a very sad situation for our children and it is only going to get worse if we do not let our politicians understand that enough is enough.

At the high school level, students are presented with more options, but these options have also been subject to cuts and restructuring due to the standardized test movement. No longer do the districts fund the sports, the performing arts organizations, and clubs that are a part of the high school curriculum (And I place these organizations as part of the curriculum because they truly help a student to learn and grow as a human being). The sponsors, the coaches, and the participants of the organization are responsible for raising the money to help keep their organization going. Again, I bring up the point—where are tax dollars going? Why are we allowing our politicians to use our tax dollars in the private sector and not for the academic and physical development of our students? A lot of extra time is being taken away from the organization because of the time needed to perform the fund-raising tasks. I have seen some programs actually removed as a part of the school's extracurricular activities because they could not raise the money to survive. This should not be an option. If there are individuals who want to participate then our tax dollars should fund it. As an example, my school used to offer sports like crew, boys and girls gymnastics and slow pitch softball with plenty of participants for each sport. When the state budget got tight for a couple years, these sports were eliminated for the purpose of saving money. You cannot tell me the money was not there it just went to some outside private source. Now there are private gymnastics organizations all over the state charging a lot of money for participants. There are club crew organizations all over the town that charge a pretty hefty penny to be a part of. There all kinds of softball organizations in town that make a lot of money from our students. Parents have accepted this and contribute lots of money to these organizations when in fact these activities should have been offered at the high school level. Why are my tax dollars being used to build an airport for some politician to fly his chartered plane rather than for my daughter to be able to participate in a sport like gymnastics or slow pitch softball? Another thing to think about is the fact there a lot of children who do not get to participate in these sports because their parents cannot afford the fees, but if these sports were offered at the high school they would be able to participate. The sad thing is our politicians have pushed the financial responsibility of our extracurricular activities back on the public. This should infuriate all of us who pay taxes. The real reason for the financial burden on parents for extracurricular activities is not because of lack of funds, but due to the misappropriation of funds to sources not deserving of the money. If I am not mistaken, it was, it should be, and it always will be our state and federal government's responsibility to provide for our children's education. Extracurricular activities are a huge part of this educational process for our students and therefore should be funded by the state, local, and federal governments.

Why has this happened? If you think about it, this has been an ongoing process by which our politicians and the business sectors have realized they can manipulate the public and reassign our tax dollars to undeserving sources. Just look at how the politicians have used the media to manipulate the public into thinking the only way to save money is through the cuts in education. Here is my theory on how politicians have tricked us into thinking there is less money for education. It starts one year with politicians claiming there is shortage in the budget and cuts will have to be made. Politicians feed the media with information about the shortage and the media prints stories, which convince the public that shortage exists. Politicians then claim one area to make up for the shortage is to cut education. All the while that this is happening, money is being redirected by our politicians to their campaign contributor's interests. This process is repeated year after year while politicians are taking money from education only to redirect it to some source of personal interest. Very rarely do you hear the media mention information about tax dollars being spent on private campaign contributor's interest. I do not know if this is because the information is not available or if the media is just part of the problem. I do know that the taxpayers have a right to know exactly where the money is going and be able to make a decision on whether it is a legitimate expenditure or not. We have allowed our politicians to feel as though they are not answerable to anyone. These cuts in education are not necessary and it trickles down to the district level forcing them to make decisions on where to cut funds. And the first area to receive a financial overhaul is the extracurricular activities. Politicians have used all kinds of scare tactics to influence the public that state and district governments do not have the money to pay for our students' extracurricular activities. This is an injustice and I would like any politician who has petitioned for money for their campaign contributors to justify this expense over funding for the public educational system. Hey wake up! These are our children and they deserve to have first consideration on any and all tax dollars from our politicians.

CHAPTER 6

PARENTAL INVOLVEMENT

Something that always seems to be a dead issue or an ignored issue whenever education reform is mentioned is the involvement parents have with their sons' or daughters' education. I honestly believe politicians stay away from this issue because they do not want to offend their potential voters. In the process, politicians have created a situation where a good majority of parents feel it is the school's and the teacher's job to raise their sons and daughters. Parents however want the schools to perform this task under a gray area where rules and laws are to be used for their own personal satisfaction. Now please understand, I am trying to emphasize the point that parents of today tend to use education, schools, and teachers as an excuse for difficulties they are experiencing with their children because politicians and NEAs have made it an easy thing to do. The law and its courts have been used by parents to intimidate and bully NEAs into making decisions that go way out of bounds from what has been previously decided. The laws I am referring to have been created to protect and support a certain class of students who are in need of special accommodations and specially trained teachers. There are however, a group of parents who have found a way to manipulate the system to compensate for their inability to parent their child. This particular group of parents recognizes the increase in NEAs and their lack of backbone and uses this to their advantage. Politicians have created such paranoia about standardized testing that parents have completely forgotten about the total education of their sons or daughters. In this standardized testing world, parents have accepted the process of teaching to pass the test and allow politicians with no educational background whatsoever to decide what should be learned. Technological advancements in education have been numerous and important but I think they have created a situation that allows parents to become less of a factor in their children's education. Having your child sit in front of a computer and learn has become an easy and common parental technique. When you look at the education of any child, a primary factor is parental involvement. Through the years, since politicians have gained control over our educational system, I have seen more and more political decisions made that have allowed our parents to become more lackadaisical with their involvement in their child's education.

In all levels of the public school system, there is a classification for a group of students who need special attention. This classification was developed through some shape or form from the American Disabilities Act and the Individuals with Disabilities Education Act. It is and always will be an important law for students with legitimate disabilities. What our politicians and our NEAs have allowed to happen with this law is a travesty. If a student is classified as EH (Emotionally Handicapped), EBD (Emotional Behavior Disability), BED (Behavioral Emotional Disability), ESE (Exceptional Student Education), OHI (Other Health Impaired), or a lot of other capital letter titles, then they are protected by the laws of the Individuals with Disabilities Education Act. Now understand for students who have legitimate disabilities such as Downs Syndrome this law protects their right to a free education and I am not pointing a finger at these individuals. I am in full support of this law for deserving students and it has been a blessing for these students. Through the years, however, this law has been abused by a group of parents who have lost control of their child. These parents use the law to get their son or daughter classified as some type of handicap to take advantage of the benefits of the law. In other words, when a parent realizes they have lost control of their son or daughter they use the Individuals with Disabilities Act to have their child classified as emotionally handicapped and use this classification to generate an excuse for their child's discipline problems. Let me give you an example of what happened in my school. We had a male student who I will call Tom. Tom had a history of discipline issues in middle school and was suspended on numerous occasions. His mother realized she could not control him so she had him tested for an emotional disability. The school psychologist (explaining how school psychologist have damaged our schools is another book) decides Tom did have an emotional handicap and now he is protected under the IDEA law. Because Tom is now protected, he has the right to continue in high school until he is twenty-two years old and he can only be suspended for a maximum of ten days per year. In Tom's (Oh I forgot to mention when Tom enters high school at the ninth grade level he is already sixteen years old) first year of high school, he is caught tagging the school with bomb threats, which is a felony but he is protected by the law, he threatens to gut a teacher like a pig but he is suspended only for ten days, and he has numerous incidents of cussing at teachers, forging passes, and skipping classes. In his second year of high school, he continues to cuss teachers out, skip classes, and he gets caught having sex with a fourteen-year-old girl in the bathroom. Now Tom is smart; he knows he cannot be arrested for statutory rape because he has not quite turned eighteen. Tom is sent to an alternative school and the girl because she is not protected by IDEA is expelled from school. It has to be mentioned that the girl was not a discipline problem in her classes and up to this point had never been suspended from school. All of Tom's infractions are reviewed by a district administrator and every time the district administrator does not and will not kick Tom out of school. Meanwhile Tom, because he is protected by IDEA, continues to come to school and influence teachers and other students in a negative way and he gets to do this until he is twenty-two years of age. Now really think about this—would you want your son or daughter in school with this type of individual? The underlying problem that our NEAs don't see is Tom is a bad kid and there is very little that is going to change that. If you look at a high school with an enrollment of 1,500 students, there are at least two hundred students that are right on the fence with their behavior of being good or bad. If a student like Tom is allowed to stay in school, he will influence at least 25 percent of those borderline students and cause them to journey on the wrong side of the fence. This in turn creates more problems for teachers in the classroom and administrators and their ability to keep the school safe. This is only one case and I promise you there are numerous others in every school in this country because parents are manipulating the system and they know that NEAs do not have the backbone or the experience to stand up and make good, sound educational decisions. The real problem in my eyes deals with NEAs and their lack of experience in knowing how a student like Tom affects the whole student population. Because of this lack of educational experience, parents can manipulate them and make the teacher look like the bad guy. The NEA looks at a student like Tom as the victim, lets him back in school, and in a few days he has influenced a number of individuals in a negative way. I have been involved when a student is caught with drugs and the parents come in and the first words out of their mouth is, my child is ESE. I mean seriously, are they not even concerned that their son or daughter is using or providing drugs to other students. The problem with the law is it is written in a generalized format, which allows the different states and local school districts to interpret its meaning differently. When you have NEAs performing their interpretation of the law it becomes a tool for parents to use when they cannot control their son or daughter.

Speaking of the lack of backbone in NEAs, parents know and can feel when they have an administrator with very little experience. If there is one thing I have learned in the profession of education, whether you are teacher or an administrator, you cannot fake experience as an educator. Parents in this day and time know most of the administrators at the schools are inexperienced and they use this to their advantage. It is amazing to me that when a student goes home and tells his or her parents that a teacher embarrassed him or her in front of the class for some disciplinary issue, the parents complain to a NEA and the administrator reprimands the teacher for being insensitive. What is hard to understand is that the NEAs of today do not even concern themselves with finding out the facts of the situation; they automatically assume the teacher is at fault. Now through this whole process, what gets lost is that the student obviously did something wrong in the classroom to warrant a disciplinary action from the teacher. The educational administrator should have expressed to the parent the need to talk to the teacher first to get the teacher's side of the story and then make a judgment as to what should be the next course of action. This is what has been lost in today's world of NEAs. Either by their own thoughts on the situation or by some directive sent down by the district office, NEAs assume the teacher is the cause of the situation. And the really sad thing is teachers are not allowed to defend themselves by asking questions; they are supposed to sit back and wait for someone at the district level to perform an investigation and make a decision. I saw one of my good friends go through this unfair process and almost give up teaching. During the change of classes, my fellow teacher was standing out by his classroom door like he is supposed to. Right down the hall from his door a fight broke out between two girls and he went to break it up while another teacher went and called for administration. I had come down the hall and saw my friend holding off both girls and they were still kicking and swinging at each other even with my friend between them. I ran and pulled one of the girls away and my friend held on to the more violent of the two. As he held her she was still kicking and swinging and I am sure he was struck multiple times by her. Finally, administration got there and took the girls away. Two days later, I saw my friend and he looked as though the whole world has caved in on him. I came to understand that the parents of the girl whom he was restraining filed charges against him for excessive force and he was being taken out of the classroom until the investigation was complete. You need to understand there were teachers and students who witnessed this man not using excessive force to restrain this female. There were video cameras in the hallway that videotaped the incident and clearly showed that he did not use excessive force and here was my friend being shown guilty until proven innocent. Not one bit of support was he shown by the district. As a matter of fact, he was told he could not say anything to anybody and they would let him know when they were done. He waited almost three weeks until the district finally made him aware of what had transpired. He was told he could go back into the classroom and he did not need to discuss it with anyone. My friend decided to do a little investigation on his own and found out that the district had settled the case rather than fight for what was right. He also found out that the whole incident would be a permanent mark on his file. My friend told me this incident was the worst time he had ever spent in his entire life. I have watched many teachers go through this process and the not knowing is extremely painful and difficult to handle. This is what we have come to—teachers are guilty until proven innocent. And I am not quite sure that once a teacher is proven innocent, if the whole thing is wiped clean from a teacher's file or whether it lingers and can be used at a later date.

I can remember never complaining to my parents about a teacher or a coach because my parents always supported the teacher or coach. My parents expected me to work hard in the classroom and be extremely respectful to my teachers or coaches. These expectations my parents held for me was pretty common with all the parents of that time. Parents of the 1960s, 1970s, and early 1980s supported the teachers, the administrators, and the school. Parents of these times did not make excuses for their sons or daughters for discipline problems.

Times have changed and it is the parents, not the students, who create all the headaches for our teachers. We consistently have situations where students are caught in dishonest acts and it is the parents that make excuses and ignore the actual act itself. I was involved one year where we literally caught a white male student trying to sell drugs to students in the school. We had student witnesses who had complained and we caught the student with the drugs on his person. A deputy was involved and the search was by the law. The male parent came in and was presented with everything that was seen and found. The male parent was a lawyer and he proceeded to accuse the teacher of everything from unlawful search to planting the drugs on the student. It was absolutely amazing. The NEA got so intimidated he let the student off on three days of in-school suspension. The deputy, the other teacher, and I were disgusted with what the NEA decided and walked out of the meeting shaking our heads. It seems that within the school system of today all a parent has to do is threaten to sue and the nonacademic personnel within a school system would shudder and give in to the parents demands. When are we going to force these parents to abide by the same rules as everyone else? When are we going to have individuals at the district level say enough is enough?

Just recently, I had an incident where I gave a test in AP statistics and the next day I received an e-mail from the assistant principal saying the mother is accusing me of not giving this student enough time to complete the test. The mother claims the student has a 504 plan and it calls for extra time on tests. The assistant principal and I have never seen such a plan for this student and when I went back and looked at the test the student had answered zero questions in a fifty-two minute period. I really do not believe that the extra time would have helped. Another incident I have to bring up involves cheating to the point of where it should be a felony. In our district, we have a computer program that teachers use to input and calculate grades. It is supposed to be a secure site with only teachers and administrators being able to access it with a district username and password. A student whose parent is an administrator at another school somehow got in to the system and changed not only her grades but several other students' grades. The student was intelligent enough to change quarter grades and semester grades so they were not as easily noticeable. A teacher noticed a change in the grades in her class and reported it to the administration. This is where it gets a little disheartening. An investigation was performed by our school administration and the culprit was found. During this whole time, the teachers of this student were never informed of any of the events that took place or were taking place. As a matter of fact, to this day the teachers of this student have never been told about the grade changes and anytime a teacher asks what is going on the reply is that the administration is handling it. After about three weeks, the teachers learned that the student was only suspended for ten days and would return to our classrooms. We needed to provide make-up work for the student. This student is still going to walk for graduation and furthermore will still be able to walk as an Honor Society student. This student was also accepted to numerous colleges and universities, one of which was an Ivy league school and they were never notified of the grade changing. Also it should be noted that the decision to sweep this whole grade change scandal under the carpet was a district decision and not the decision of our school administration. Our school administration was just as disgusted, but were told the district would handle it. I guess being the child of an administrator in the district does have its advantages.

Another problem with parents of today is that they have been manipulated by our politicians into thinking their sons' or daughters' success is solely based on a standardized test score. Parents of today have lost their focus on policing their children and making sure they receive a well-rounded education. Politicians have somehow persuaded parents to believe the measure of their children's education and what their child knows is from the score of a one-day standardized test. I am not quite sure how this is happening because every parent has been through some type of educational process and I know they understand how pointless a standardized test is. Have parents become that busy or lazy in their parental duties? Standardized practice sheets have replaced creative, innovative teaching methodologies. It is pretty sad when I see elementary age students having to work a good majority of their school days on generic worksheets and not on some type of activity that stimulates creative thinking. But then again that is what our politicians want, a population that *cannot and will not think for themselves*. Politicians have made sure the pressure of passing the test and ultimately passing a grade level is felt by the parents and the parents have made sure that this same pressure is felt by the students. I have heard numerous stories of students from all levels being stressed to the point of sickness or depression. There seems to be this domino effect of standardizing everyone in our country and it is the politicians who want to be at the top, controlling the process. I see and understand the dilemma that parents are in; I only wish parents could see and understand how the politicians have manipulated them. Parents need to demand that our politicians make solid educational decisions that promote creative, independent learning, not this assembly line education that we have now. Parents need to concern themselves with the teaching methodologies in the classroom that are allowing our students to develop their own individual creative selves. Parents of the past were focused and concerned on classroom learning and how their sons and daughters were performing in the classroom. Parents of the past did not place value for their children's future on the passing of a standardized test. Parents of today have been tricked into believing a child's future is a cumulative result of a few standardized test scores through the elementary, middle, and high school years. How can the scores on a standardized test indicate a child's will to improve, will to pick themselves up and continue to work toward a goal, and their ability to create? Parents of today have lost their commitment to their child's whole education and have succumbed to a standardized education. It is time for parents of today to demand a better whole education for their sons and daughters.

Technology has also allowed parents to become less involved in their child's education. With all the grading programs there are, it makes it easy for a parent to check their son's or daughter's grade and if satisfied never have to verbally talk to them about their education. Technology has made it easy for parents to keep their children out of school and take vacations or other absentee reasons because of being able to get the make-up work through e-mail or a Web site. I feel parents have allowed their children to become less responsible for their own education because of the advancements in technology. It is the parents that generally e-mail or look on a Web site to find the make-up or missing assignments. What ever happened to the student having the responsibility of going to the teacher and asking for their own make-up work? You may think I am being a little picky here, but I know that based on the students I have taught, the ones who were the most successful are the ones who were responsible for their own education. These are the students who did not wait for someone to tell them what to do and how to do it. These are the students who did not depend on their parents to think for them. I feel parents of today have allowed themselves to think they are too busy to be available for their children. And then again I think the standardization of our public educational system has set a trap for parents into thinking they are doing the right things for their children because the media and our politicians claim it is the right way to educate their children. I really feel our politicians set up laws and mandates to keep parents from being personally involved in their children's education. Parents have the ability to talk to their sons and daughters personally not through a computer program. Parents have the ability to attend and be a part of their sons' and daughters' extracurricular activities. Parents should not let the politicians and their standardization movement prevent them from guiding their children into being creative, independent thinkers.

CHAPTER 7

LACK OF SUPPORT TO TEACHERS

THIS CHAPTER IS GOING TO get a little personal because I am going to speak from my experiences through the years and I think what you read here will reflect how a lot of teachers feel. First of all I am tired of hearing politicians and the media voice their ideas that teachers are not appreciated. The idea that teachers are not paid enough for what their job involves, that teaching is one of the most important jobs in our country—these seem to be the same old statements that come out of our politicians' mouths and yet there has never been a politician or a media individual who has ever went to bat for teachers, one hundred percent. Politicians play to the public's opinions with these types of statements long enough to get elected and then the issues in education are put to the side until the next election.

It was around 1990 that I began to notice a change in the philosophy and attitude toward teachers. Up until then I was teaching and coaching at a private catholic high school and in 1990, I was hired to teach mathematics and start the basketball program at a brand new public high school. The principal I worked for was one of the best I have encountered in my career. He always based his decisions on what was best educationally not in terms of being popular or financial limits. Gangs were becoming more of a factor because the district had downsized the middle school's extracurricular programs to almost nothing and students were looking to belong to a group, thus, the increased popularity of gang membership. One morning before school, the coaches were coming out of meeting when a student came running up to say his friend had been beaten up by a gang from another high school and the gang was still on campus. All the coaches did a remarkable job of rounding up every single one of the gang members. The principal called in the local authorities to have the gang members arrested. To send a message to any potential gang members at our school, the principal had the law officers bring the arrested gang members through the school at a change between classes. This allowed all students in the school to see and realize there will be consequences for gang-related behavior. A couple of days later, a meeting was called for all involved in the incident and we really thought we were going to be congratulated on resolving the problem so quick. When we sat down, a district administrator proceeded to belittle us and say we embarrassed the gang members (he proceeded to call them students.) and we are to never let it happen again. My principal was not present at the meeting and to make a long story short he was transferred at the end of the year. I present this story at the beginning of this chapter to set the tone for how the philosophy of our educational leaders has developed today. Since this incident, I have seen so many more incidents where the district personnel showed lack of support for teachers and educational administrators. As years have passed and the standardization of education was able to eliminate the educational principals and administration in schools, there now is very little support shown to teachers from the state, from the district office, and their own school administration.

Since this incident happened, I have seen less and less support for teachers at the state level, the district level, and the school level. At the state level, politicians have continuously tried to use the private business sector as a model for evaluating and defining a teacher's worth. Politicians want you to believe that our schools are in bad shape and it is the teaching in the classroom that is the cause. They would like you to put your trust in their abilities to run education and teachers like a business. If you look at my last statement, the word *trust* is a characteristic that is one sided; politicians want the public to trust them but they very rarely exhibit this same trust in the public. And really if you think about the schools being run like a business, aren't decisions in a business all about making money? So if we run our schools like a business, decisions will be made based on finances. Therefore, decisions are made based on the bottom line. This is what is happening in our schools. The concern for what our students are learning and the choices in the curriculum take a back seat to the dollars being spent. Can you see that all these have been the plan of our politicians to take money from educating our children and placing it in some other private source? Politicians have seen the apathy in the public and used this apathy to build their standardized educational agenda. Politicians have created this atmosphere in our public educational system that promotes the idea of producing the highest quota we can, regardless of who "gets left behind." You tell me how a young person's education can be measured by a single numerical value. Do you remember when you took a standardized test, how much did you really learn? Does it not seem obvious that our politicians want to take away the ability for our children to become free-thinking individuals and to force teachers to be workers, not educational professionals?

Because we are running our schools like a business, school administrators are interested only in the bottom line, which in education is the passing rate on the state standardized test. This means school districts will sacrifice anything to get the passing rate to increase. Individuals at the district level who have very little experience in the classroom make decisions that negatively affect the creative process of teaching. I have seen school districts spend large amounts of money on seminars from private organizations that really had very little influence on the whole education of the students. These private organizations developed programs to specifically make money and sell school districts on the idea the program will increase performance on the standardized test. In my district, someone decided all teachers in the district should read Robert J. Marzano's book *The Art and Science of Teaching*. Now I am sure Mr. Marzano is an intelligent human being but the guy was only in the high school classroom for four years and that was from 1967 to 1971. What can this guy possibly know about what is going on in the classroom in 2011? He was an English teacher, so how does he know the methodologies in teaching other subjects? The only reason the program this guy has developed is used is because you have some noneducational individual who read the book and said, "That sounds good. Let's use in our schools." And the district noneducational individual who made this decision has never been in the classroom long enough to understand what classroom teaching is all about. These programs do not help in any way to develop the long-time learning within the classroom. The programs, the books, and even the speakers are quick fixes for issues in the classroom that are constantly changing. This is always evident by the title, which usually includes some type of descriptive term about the art of, the desire of, or the science of education or learning. I just have a hard time understanding why individuals who have spent little to no time teaching in a classroom are considered experts and the public does not question the amount of money spent to these individuals. This money could have been spent directly into the classroom for supplies, equipment, and technology. This money could have been used for teachers to observe each other and learn form each other.

In the last twenty years, politicians have not put their trust in teachers and the result has been a business-like educational system that produces an assembly line, cookie cutter type of student. Teachers are the key to any good educational process. If teachers are restricted in the methodologies they are allowed to use in the classroom then the ability for a student to be a creative, independent learner can never develop. This is what is happening in this standardized movement in education. Teachers are being told items that need to be in their classrooms and where to place them. Teachers are being told how to start, continue, and finish every lesson being taught. Politicians have transformed teachers into assembly line workers producing a standardized student. I know some of you are thinking this guy is a teacher and he is just bitter. Well you are right I am bitter. I am bitter not for myself because I am at the end of my career and do not succumb to the political agenda of our supposed public servants. I am bitter for all the younger and beginning teachers who have not had the chance to experience and develop into the real creative teacher they could be. The beginning teachers of today have no clue as to how good they really could be. I am bitter because we as the public allow these self-righteous individuals who think they are above everyone else make the decisions that affect our teachers and limit a teacher's ability to grow creatively. Our politicians of today show absolutely no support for our teachers and the public school system.

Public education is not private and it is not a business. I get really angry when I hear a politician propose the voucher system for students to attend private schools. I do not know about you, but if a politician is saying we need to give up on public education and send the money to private schools, then this politician is telling me he does not want to do his job and help make our public educational system stronger, better. And really think about this—we are going to provide money for students to go to a private school that the politicians do not even require to have their students take the state standard test. How do the politicians know the private school education is better than the public schools education and why are the private schools exempt from the state standardized test? I am sorry but if politicians really were committed to making our public educational system the best, there would not be a need for private education schools. I have taught in both the private sector and the public sector and I can honestly say there is very little difference in the teachers and the education. As a matter of fact, there is very little difference in the whole educational process other than the curriculum and the fact that private schools are allowed to offer courses in theology. This debate on private versus public also helps me to see how little our politicians truly know about public education. I mean, public education is exactly what the word says, it is public (in the respect we educate everyone) but it is also personal (there is a personal individual education for each individual student). This is what truly exposes our politicians for the lack of understanding and commitment they have for the teachers. In the study by Dr. Steven L. Paine performed for the McGraw-Hill Research Foundation titled, *"What the U.S. Can Learn From the World's Most Successful Education Reform Efforts."* Dr. Paine concluded that the U.S. and its political base must raise the level of professional regard in which the job of a teacher is held. He found that in top-performing countries like Japan, South Korea, Finland, and Canada, teachers are typically paid better relative to others, education credentials are valued more, and a higher share of educational spending is devoted to instructional services. I mean, if you really think about it, if our politicians truly wanted our educational system to be the best in the world wouldn't they support legislation that would give funds to improve classroom teaching and allow our teachers to achieve higher level degrees?

My wife worked for a medical device company and she was given five thousand dollars a year to obtain an advanced educational degree. I have a friend who is an engineer and his company paid for him to receive his master's degree. Why do I bring this up? Because in education, teachers are not given the same financial consideration for pursuing advanced degrees. Politicians and district administration do not place a high value on an advanced degree that deals with a teacher's advancement personally and practically. A masters or doctorate degree in education is not looked at by our leaders as a critical stepping stone in creating more effective teachers. You would think that when you enter the field of education, there would be a constant show of support by our leaders toward achieving a higher level of education. You would think politicians and district administrators would want all of their teachers to attain the highest level of education possible. There would be money and incentives to support teachers in their pursuit of a higher level degree. This is not the case, and I honestly believe it is because our politicians and the district administrators want the teachers to stay at a certain intellectual level. Masters and doctorate courses are developed to push the student to think and create outside the general boundaries of their educational discipline. This is what our politicians and our district administrators do not want to see. They do not want teachers to gain intellectual confidence and begin to question the politicians' lack of educational knowledge. If teachers begin to question politicians at a higher intellectual level, the politicians lose control of the standardization they have worked so hard to create. What politicians and district administrators have done is spend money on in-service or professional service activities that are standardized and do not develop a teachers ability to be more confident in their teaching methodologies. Politicians have spent money on promoting a program called board-certified teacher and it is within itself a political side show. Programs like board-certified teacher are ineffective and do not help a teacher improve his or her educational personal practices.

I honestly believe the reason in-service or professional service activities is used is that the politicians and the district want to have control over what they want the teachers to be exposed to. Talk to any teacher from any state and I guarantee they would rather spend their time pursuing a higher level degree than sitting in an in-service activity learning very little. Right now teachers are being bombarded by an overabundance of these in-service activities and all they do is continually remind teachers that their leadership has very little faith in them. These activities attempt to influence teachers into teaching the same thing, the same way, at the same time. I can remember the last in-service I attended dealt with constructing word walls. The whole point of the presentation was high school teachers should have a certain area of their walls with words and their definitions for students to look at during class. The word wall is supposed to help the students learn the definitions. Now I can see this being somewhat helpful at the elementary level, but can you imagine one of my AP statistics seniors going to his first college class and asking the professor where her word wall is? I am sorry but this is another poor idea from a noneducational individual and the sad thing is it undermines the teacher and waters down the whole educational process. I mean, why should a student put the effort into learning the words if he or she knows the words are going to be up on the wall? Another brilliant idea coming from our district office is the idea of learning goals. In theory, this idea sounds really effective; in practice, it is not very practical. A learning goal is acceptable if you want to teach one dimensionally. The real art of teaching involves standing in front the classroom and reading the students faces, their questions, and their actions to understand exactly the road to go down to facilitate learning. What you have to understand is this art of teaching changes from class to class and day to day. The real art of teaching is adapting to help every individual student in every class have the opportunity to learn. The learning-goal process is another process that sounds really good on paper but when you take the idea in the classroom it restricts the teachers' ability to adapt. As stated previously in this book, I believe politicians want our students to be factory-line learners and they want our teachers to be factory-line workers. Hey, is this not the business approach of CEOs (politicians) at the top controlling the employees (teachers) to produce the same product (standardized students)? By this I mean they want all of our students to have to be dependent on being told how to study and how to learn. They want all of our teachers to be dependent on being told what to teach, when to teach, and how to teach. Politicians do not want our teachers or our students to be creative, independent thinkers because then they will be questioned on every decision they make.

In 1987, an independent, nonpartisan, nonprofit, nongovernmental company came up with the idea of board-certified teachers. This company charged x-amount of dollars for teachers to go through a series of requirements and when the requirements were satisfied, they were given the title of board certified. The state contributed most of the money involved and on top of it gave teachers extra dollars on their salaries for completion of the process. I have a couple of points I would like to address about this. First, the process was a dog-and-pony show that even the worst of teachers could complete and receive the board-certified teacher title. The process consists of a submitted portfolio in which the participating teacher has to present evidence of classroom-based entries (as they are called by the National Board for Professional Teaching Standards). These classroom entries involved one classroom-based entry with student work, two videos of lessons with student interaction, and one accomplishment outside the classroom, and how it benefits students in the classroom. Herein lies the problem—all of the entries are organized by the participating teacher with no one from the organization actually coming into the classroom to see if the video entries are in fact true on a day-to-day basis. Teachers are able to video their best-case scenario and make sure everything is in proper order. The second component to the certification involves a participating teacher demonstrating content knowledge in response to six exercises developed for a chosen certification area. The teacher would perform this part of process at one of three hundred computers located across the United States. Again I would like to point out there is no personal contact between the teacher and the organization. Explain to me how this process defines a better teacher in the classroom. How does having a portfolio with lessons I have selected and the answers to six content knowledge questions justify me being a better teacher? Yet our politicians spent a lot of money on this very process. It makes me think that some politicians or politician had a vested interest in this company. Besides, why not spend all this money on teachers and their advancement to a masters or doctorate degree unless you do not want your teachers to become intellectually and educationally stronger?

The lack of teacher support is most evident in the way politicians have changed the emphasis from classroom practices and classroom learning to the theory that every subject should be taught with the same set of methods at the same time for exactly the same result for every student. Now think about what you just read especially the last part about the same result for every student. Remember, when you were in school and you got to experience many different teaching styles, some styles agreed with your learning style and some did not. Think back to those teachers that you really connected with and how they influenced your life. Think back to the teachers that you did not connect with and how they influenced your life. The point is, you and I got to experience teachers for who they really were good or bad and gained knowledge about ourselves on how we liked to learn. The students of today do not get to experience this because there is no support at the state or district level for a teacher's individual creative teaching styles. The state puts demands on the district and the district requires these same demands on their teachers. Every year teachers are being restricted more and more from being creative in their teaching methodologies in the classroom. The state and the district have made it clear that they are more capable of deciding the methodologies to be used when teaching in the classroom even though there is very little educational experience at the state and district levels. It is the same condescending attitude that politicians, media, and all other professions show toward teachers. An example of the condescending attitude that other professions have of teachers is in the movie *Prince of Tides* starring Nick Nolte and Barbara Streisand. In the movie, Streisand plays a psychologist who is treating Nolte's sister. Nolte is an English teacher/football coach from the state of South Carolina. Streisand has a son who wants to play football at his private school, so Streisand asks Nolte if he will tutor her son in football. Nolte agrees to the job and Streisand asks how much he will charge. Nolte responds by asking Streisands character how much she charges her patients. When Streiand tells him the amount Nolte tells her that this amount will be fine. Streisand's look is priceless and it sums up the condescending attitude that she has about what she really thinks of Nolte's value as a teacher. Nolte sees the look and says something like you do not believe my expertise in football is worth the same as your expertise in psychology. This is a typical feeling with individuals who consider themselves above the teaching profession. Politicians are the absolute, worse offenders. I really believe they see teaching as a menial job that anyone can do and not as a profession. This is why it is so easy for them to cut funds from education. I recognize teaching as one of the most important professions in our country and it is a profession that a lot of individuals such as politicians cannot perform. Yet teachers are treated as if they are second class in the professional work force. You see, I think we have this whole thing backward because I am pretty sure I could do a politician's job (definitely with more honesty and integrity) but I know they could not do my job in the classroom. So we should consider a politician's job as being a job that anyone can perform. I mean seriously, we have had an actor as president of the United States and he did a pretty good job.

Have you noticed the one issue that is always mentioned when education reform is discussed is teacher merit pay? Have you also noticed there has never been a successful merit teacher plan ever executed? Sure there have been plans that survive for a year or two, but there are always variables that arise later and create controversy. Politicians are notorious for supporting teacher merit pay, but have you ever seen a politician with a step-by-step working model for merit pay other than the results of standardized test scores? The reason you have not is because the politicians know it is an impossible task to use a business evaluation model to recognize effective teaching practices. Here is why the practice of teaching cannot be treated like a business. In a business, employees are judged or evaluated based on the profits a business accumulates in a calendar year. The CEOs or individuals at the top only look at the profit numbers and if there are unacceptable numbers in some part of the business, then there are changes in those areas that the higher ups in the company feel will produce more profits. Generally, changes within a business usually result in an individual or individuals being replaced to see if the new individuals can produce more profit. Because all of the employees are basically on annual contracts the higher ups can repeat this process of replacement as much as they choose until they find someone who makes the final numbers rise. In this whole process, there is no concern about the product's self-esteem, its ability to improve, its ability to pick itself up from being knocked down and continue to go through life because most of the products in business are not young human beings. Politicians feel we can base merit pay on standardized test scores and use these standardized test scores along the same lines as a business uses production numbers. The business model is not for education due to the human factor. What I mean by the human factor is our product in education is a human being who has learned enough academically to function as a positive force to himself or herself and society. Understand our goal in education is not to produce a bunch of individuals who can score high enough one time on a standardized test. Our goal as teachers is to produce individual human beings who have high self-esteem, who can problem solve in their area of interest, and who are solid citizens. Where is the concern from our politicians in these areas of development for our students? Why are our politicians not addressing these issues about our children's education?

What type of incentive do students have to perform well on a standardized test? You might say the students are able to graduate to the next level, but I am sorry to inform you that is not an incentive; it is a threat. And think about this, when you took a standardized test how much of the information did you retain? You know you worked to pass the test not to learn and retain the material. Where is the incentive? There is also the problem with absenteeism. In a business, if you are continually absent from work, your supervisor will eventually fire you. In education, teachers cannot fire students from the classroom. Teachers have to devise strategies to help truant students catch up. Now let's also realize that a student does not have to be physically absent from class to be absent from class. How do you measure effort? I have seen students who worked their tail off to receive a C in my class and other students who barely put in the effort and received an A. Who really deserves the A? Where is effort measured on a standardized test?

CHAPTER 8

WHERE IS ALL THE MONEY GOING?

I HAVE SPECIFICALLY LEFT THIS information as the last chapter because it is a topic that is not only a concern with our educational system but with all other legitimate entities that rely on funding from federal, state, and local politicians. When you look at the pool of money that our public educational system is supposed to be funded from, you have to wonder why there is such a drastic shortage. In any particular state in the union, funding for education is supposed to come from multiple sources such as real estate taxes, lotto money, sales tax, state income tax, and luxury taxes. I do not know the exact dollars that come from a particular source and I have yet to see a spreadsheet describing or explaining the amount of dollars each source produces. Let's take a look at each one of these sources and look at the possible theoretical dollars. Now remember this is purely theoretical and the purpose is for you to see that there is no way there ever should be a shortage in funds for our students and their education.

Let's look at real estate taxes first. In any state, real estate taxes are collected from personal homeowners and businesses who own real property. The amount of homes and buildings is probably proportional to population size of the state with the exception of states that house a large amount of illegal aliens. In these states, the real property is probably slightly proportionally less than the population size. Now if you think about it, a certain percentage of property taxes is always supposed to go to public education and that percentage is adjusted based on property values. Most school districts or counties figure a budget and then come up with a mileage rate that is supposed to financially support their predictions for the new school year. Right here, I hope you can see that our school systems should be starting with a fair amount of funds to cover their number of students being predicted for the next school year. This should allow our schools to be able to operate at an efficient level, providing for classroom supplies, district payroll, and maintenance on school properties. Just from real estate taxes there should be enough funds to start a school year with a positive outlook. If schools have qualified individuals to calculate the numbers correctly then the real estate taxes should allow district administrators to budget money in the right areas for the right reasons.

The second source at which schools are supposed to receive funds from is at the state level and includes state and local sales tax, state income tax, and/or luxury taxes. These funds are in addition to the real estate taxes mentioned earlier. The amount of money that comes from these state taxes varies from year to year and is in addition to any local real estate tax funds. A local government can ask the citizens of their district or county to impose a higher sales tax rate for the sole purpose of funding their public educational system. In any particular year, the public educational systems should be able to rely on a certain percentage of funds coming from state taxes and use this money in addition to what has already been budgeted from the local real estate taxes. At this point, our school systems should now have enough funds to operate without concern over any type of unanticipated expense such as increased student enrollment, unexpected repairs to buildings or vehicles, and increased expense for supplies. The amount of money coming from both of the above-mentioned sources should allow our public schools to maintain an operational level that is as good, if not better, than the previous year. I hope that you understand the theoretical mathematics. If the real estate taxes and state taxes are budgeted in a fair and honest procedure, our public educational systems are prospering, not scraping to survive. Just with these two sources, the public educational systems should have the money to maintain a high quality of education in the classroom and in extracurricular activities.

Now we come to the third and final source of funds to public education, which almost every state now has and that is the lottery system. I remember when the lottery system was introduced to the public, politicians emphasized the point that the money from lottery would enhance educational spending and not replace it. So the public thinking they could believe their politicians voted for the lottery system. If you think about the amount of money that is generated through all lottery games and the fact that our politicians promised the money would be used to supplement education, we should have the most well-funded educational system in the world. The lottery funds are supposed to be in addition to the real estate taxes and the state taxes. Let me give you a few mathematical ideas on the amount of money generated through lottery games. First, the jackpot prize is always fifty percent of what is actually collected. This means that if the jackpot is 10 million the state has collected 20 million. A winner must always pay taxes on the money won and because lottery winnings are usually large amounts of money, the government collects a certain percentage of the winnings due to taxes. In the scratch off games there is a certain statistical concept called expected value. The expected value is the amount of money the owner of the game expects to pay out per ticket. If the owner of the game is out to make money, the expected payout is usually 50 percent of the ticket price. So if we take a five-dollar scratch off ticket, the expected payout is probably around two dollars and fifty cents, which means the government is making two dollars and fifty cents on every ticket sold. Other things to consider are the uncollected prizes and where that money goes. What I am trying to help you understand is the amount of money that is generated through the lottery system and it is all supposed to be for education. If you look at the three sources of funds that are supposed to be given to run our public educational system, I hope you can visualize the large amount of money that should be there.

Where is all this money? How have politicians manipulated these funds so there is a shortage of money for our children and their education? Here is my take on this problem. We have not made our politicians accountable for all of these funds, so they are taking money from these sources to help satisfy the debts they owe to their large campaign contributors. Politicians realized sometime ago they could sell the public on generating more money for our public educational system through alternative sources such as the lottery games. The money from the alternative sources allows the politicians to be able to cut the amount of state dollars to education and replace it with lottery dollars. Politicians can then take the cut educational dollars and channel toward their special interests. Why do we never see a complete breakdown of where exactly all our dollars go? Politicians do not allow us to see this type of data because they know how angry it would make us. This is why businesses and special interests groups spend so much money on getting certain individuals elected. This is why lobbyists have become just as prominent at any state capitol as the politicians themselves. So if we really think about it, if there is a business that needs some 2 million dollars to fund a project, this business can spend let say 100,000 dollars getting Joe Politician elected and in turn Joe Politician makes sure the business gets their 2 million dollars from the taxpayers. Not to mention Joe Politician owes this business for the rest of his political career. Not a bad return on the businesses' investment. And if you think of almost every politician that is at the local, state, or federal level and the favors they owe, no wonder there is little money left for our public educational system. Can you imagine being the CEO of a major corporation and using tax dollars to fund some of your major projects? You will definitely look good in the eyes of the stock holders.

It does not stop at the lottery because when the politicians begin to spend more money with outside private sources than the lottery takes in they have to go after other sources of funds. This is happening right now in my state and probably a lot other states in the country. I know there is no particular set of funds that are safe from our noble politicians, but I am only going to concentrate on funds that deal with education. In the state of Florida, politicians have done a remarkable job of making the pension for educators, police officers, and firemen look as though it is costing the taxpayers an enormous amount of money. My question is why all of a sudden did the pension for these individuals just now become such a burden? The answer is in the earlier paragraph. It is not the cost of the pensions for these individuals that is the problem, it is the way our politicians have been careless in the distribution of tax funds to the private sector. Politicians have exhausted their slush funds such as lottery, and in order to keep their promises to their major campaign contributors, they have to find the money from other governmental sources. This is where the politicians and the media jump in bed with each other and deceive the public with negative publicity. If you ever notice, it is always the same trick with the media as the media presents a worst-case scenario involving not a teacher but a noneducational administrator who truly has abused the system with numbers that would make anyone jealous including the teachers themselves. The media does a good job of influencing the public into thinking that all teachers are receiving the same amount of money. Teachers, police officers, and firemen deserve the pensions because of the jobs they are required to perform. Have we forgotten these individuals start their professions with a mediocre salary and have to work for twenty to thirty years in order to receive their pensions? The abuse that has been so widely publicized in the media with pensions does not involve the teachers, police officers, or firemen but their administrative higher ups. It really upsets me when I see and hear some television personality talk about the pensions and how these individuals do not deserve them. These individuals from the media are either ignorant or have some vested interest in the politicians and therefore want to influence in a way that allows the current politicians or ones like them to continue to make the financial decisions that are bankrupting this country. In all the talk about pensions for teachers, firemen, and police officers, I have never heard one solid financial explanation other than the budget is short on money. By the way who are the individuals that created this lack of funds? Politicians are masters at deceiving the public and controlling information that is presented to the public. Politicians have used educational funds for far to long to supplement their careless spending year after year..

When you really think of the fact that our tax dollars are supposed to pay for and run our public educational system, it should become very clear that we should never and I mean never have a shortage of funds for our children. It is our politicians at all levels that use the same practice of thinking about their commitments or favors they owe first, making sure there is enough money to cover their preelection debts. After their preelection debts are taken care of, they use the left-over money to budget for education. In the process, there is not enough money to cover the expenses needed to run the public educational system and our politicians begin to attack certain government agencies so the politicians can cut their individual budgets and use the money to make up the difference of what they have budgeted for, their campaign promises, or favors. I hope you understand the math here. It is not that public education has gotten to be the financial burden that our politicians would like us to believe in; it is simply the fact that our politicians have spent our tax dollars in a whole lot of the wrong places. If we continue to let our politicians follow this practice of budgeting funds to people, organizations and companies that truly do not need the money, our politicians will deplete every dime of our public educational system. I cannot stress it enough we need to make our politicians be more accountable and open to allowing the public to see where every penny of our tax dollars is being spent. If we truly want the best educational system for our children, then we need to make sure our politicians understand how our tax dollars should be budgeted. As I have said previously in this book, the two most important groups of people who should always be considered first on any budget for any year are our children and our seniors. This is not happening with the greedy career politicians we have today.

CONCLUSION

In CLOSING, I WOULD LIKE to give my opinion of the future of education and the profession of teaching if no measures are taken against the political powers. As I started to write this chapter of the book, there are already a lot of political decisions being passed in different states that are going to drastically affect education and teachers. In Florida, politicians have just passed a merit pay plan that has no plan and no money to pay the teachers. Florida has also decided to balance the budget on the backs of teachers by eliminating their pensions. In Wisconsin and Indiana, the governors have decided to eliminate collective bargaining despite strong protests from the public and other state politicians. In other states, there are numerous cuts and the elimination of certain programs that the public has no input on. All of the decisions being made are politically and financially motivated at the expense of our educational system. I cannot remember the last time a politician actually campaigned with the idea of increasing the money budgeted to education. It seems to me politicians only know one real truth when it comes to education and that is the truth of being able to bleed education little by little until there is only a fragment of what we once had. Think of the educational system you went through and compare it to what the children of today have. When I ask you to think of your education, I am asking you to think of the freedom you had in selecting your courses, the different styles of teaching you experienced (good and bad), and the extracurricular activities you were allowed to experience from elementary years into your high school years. Children of today are being shortchanged in their overall public education by a political system that is greedy and dishonest. If we continue to allow our politicians to be the sole decision makers in the financial and curricular development of our public educational system, we will see and experience complete elimination of a free public education.

You will see politicians continue to convince the public that there is less and less money for education without any type of numerical explanation. The whole purpose of this tactic is to eventually bring public education to a point were it is no longer free. This is already starting to happen with families having to pay a fee to their children's school for such things as supplies, science, and pay to play or participate in extracurricular activities. There used to be money that supported athletic teams, performing arts organizations, and supplies in schools. Through the reduction of budgets by our politicians school districts have been forced to pass those expenses on to the parents or to the organizations themselves. Please understand what I am saying. Politicians have told our schools, our teachers, and our students through the last fifteen years that they need to sacrifice monies owed to them to help balance the local, state, and federal budgets. All the while, politicians continue to take money from our public educational system and ask parents to pick up the difference; they (politicians) themselves have sacrificed nothing. As a matter of fact, the politicians continue to give themselves the best of benefits and raises on their salaries. Politicians have told the local school districts they will be decreased by X amount of dollars and this in turn causes the school districts to impose financial decisions that affect our schools, teachers, and students in negative ways. Politicians in this day and time are bought and paid for by outside sources and these outside sources are the parasites that feed off of the tax dollars that are supposed to go the education of our children. I truly believe there is always enough money to fund our public educational system to be the best in the world. Politicians, however, have found the money budgeted for education to be a plentiful source of payback funds to their outside sources. Have you not noticed how politicians continue to cut funds to different aspects of our educational system year after year but never mention any decrease in funding to their outside sources? I would just like to know where all of our tax dollars go in an honest itemized statement.

Technology in public education is being pushed more and more each year by our political leaders. Sure, you can say public education is better because of all the advancements in technology, but has the technology really created a better learning environment or has technology allowed our politicians to control the education our children receive? In the old days, teachers made their test or quiz so each test or quiz was an individual creation from that teacher. Generally, the test could not be duplicated unless it was stolen from the teacher's desk. With today's technology all teachers teaching the same subject have the same computer resources with the same testing materials. This means that if the same book is adopted in every county in the state, then every teacher teaching that course uses the same tests, quizzes, and possibly the same worksheets. This allows students to post the test answers on the Internet or any other technological communicating source. Technology has made it easy for students to not have to study and learn the material. Here is an example, in my AP statistics class, I have numerous worksheets, practice tests, quizzes, and tests and I have restructured them from time to time to eliminate cheating from year to year. One day after what I thought was a challenging test that I personally constructed, a student came to me and said the test scores are going to be really good. At that time, I did not think anything of it until I started grading the test and the scores were really high and answers to particular problems had the same wording. The next day after class I asked the same student how she knew the scores would be high. She responded with a simple reply of "cell phones." Later I found out that students were taking pictures of the test questions and answers on their cell phones and sending to students who not taken the test yet. Technology has made it convenient to not have to study. And call it a conspiracy theory but I honestly believe politicians are okay with the cheating because our students stay within that standardized structure and are easy to manipulate as adults.

Technology has made it easy for politicians to control the information and material that our public educational systems are allowed to use. I am really tired of all the political correctness that has been shoved on us because of the advancements in technology. Politicians and nonacademic district administrators are using technology to censorinformation that teachers, academic administrators receive and are able to transmit. I do not think that our forefathers really intended for a select few individuals to control the information that everyone else receives. And in education, the select individuals control what our students are allowed to learn. Look at the textbooks we are using today; they are written with standardization in mind. They are written to sell copies, which means they are written to satisfy our politicians and the standardized education the politicians promote. The textbooks of today are written not only with controlled information but also written to reduce the amount of independent thinking. I really think this is exactly what our politicians would like to see—a society that cannot or will not think for themselves. This would give certain families rights to political positions. Have you noticed that politics has become a family business?

Education is not a thing you can force on someone. Sure, the politicians and the district nonacademic administrators (NEAs) can pass laws or rules that force an individual to be at a particular educational facility, but they cannot and I emphasize cannot guarantee an individual will learn. Learning is an action that has to be a desire of the individual. And because of the many, many differences we have in our human population we have many, many different levels of desire. Unfortunately, in this politically controlled educational time, desire is not a factor considered to be important when it comes to standardized education. In this standardized era, we have a lot of individuals leaving our schools who have not learned a damn thing. These individuals are disinterested in the information that a standardized test is composed of. The academic information in this standardized system is a cookie cutter formula to produce an individual who does not have a clue of where their talents and interests are and how to think for themselves. We have the students at the top who are so bored with the level of academic material in the standardized movement that they waste half of their academic career just getting through it. We have the students in the middle who learn just enough to pass the test to move on. The standardized material does create an environment for these students to think outside the box so they generally pass the test, walk out, and forget about any material associated with the standardized test. Then there is the bottom twenty-five percent who really have no interest whatsoever in a standardized test. And as I have previously mentioned in an early chapter of this book, these are the students that suffer the most from a standardized public school system because of the lack of availability of courses that help these students learn vocational skills. I do not know exactly where the quote came from and I am sure I will not say exactly in the same form as the original author but it goes something like this "Power is keeping the masses strong in body and weak in mind." I honestly believe this is the goal our politicians have to keep themselves in their political offices for a long time.

It is education that defines a society and our American educational system is the best in the world. Politicians and NEAs need to keep a very far distance away from our educational system. It is teachers, students, and parents who have been and always will be the foundation and framework of our American public educational system. Our teachers are the absolute best in the world and I am tired of seeing and hearing politicians and the media continually bash the profession.

For too long, politicians have used a small number of incompetent teachers to be representative of all teachers. This is not only unfair but an indication of how our politicians really devalue the profession of teaching. Our teachers care about the education of their students and they work extremely hard to help students have the best possible chance to learn. It is the teachers with multiple years of experience in the classroom who have developed their teaching personal practical theories and are now the positive force our students need. Experienced teachers are experienced because they want to be in the classroom. They enjoy being around their students and the experienced teachers take a lot of pride in watching their students develop, not from a standardized approach but a humanistic, cognitive approach. These are the teachers that can stand up in front of a classroom and adapt to the educational situation as it changes from minute to minute, student to student. It is the teachers of experience that the politicians are trying to drive away because politicians know these are the teachers that see through their noneducational decisions. It is the teachers of experience that need to speak out and expose the politicians and the NEAs for their lack of educational experience and their lack of support to America's educational system. Just as I have stated about politicians wanting students who cannot think for themselves, these same politicians want teachers who have to be told what to teach, how to teach it, and when to teach it. Think of how much power and how much control our politicians will have if they continue to control our educational system. They control the information that is learned in school so they control the public's interpretation of their job performance.

What has gotten lost through this whole political educational phase is the responsibility our politicians have in funding and supporting our schools, our teachers, and our students. As I write this last chapter, the United States of America is going through a Presidential election and I am appalled at the amount of money the candidates are raising for their campaigns. There are students all across this country whose families are homeless, whose families don't have enough money to clothe or feed their children for school, whose families don't have the resources to make sure their children are receiving all possible advantages for a strong education. And yet we have politicians who have millions sometimes billions of dollars just to campaign. Is there something truly wrong with that picture? I am sure the politicians are not receiving their campaign dollars from individuals like you and me, so were does it come from? Let's see if it is not coming from the average U.S. family then the contributions must be coming from the businesses, corporations, and special interests groups that have alternative motives that have absolutely nothing to do with the education of our children. Now this means our politicians are not committed to the people who actually voted and elected them, but campaign contributors that are requesting favors. This is why the tax dollars, the lotto dollars, and any other dollars that come into the government are slowly dwindling down and away from our public educational system. As I have stated earlier when an individual is elected to serve the masses, the first two groups of individuals that should be taken care of are our children and our older generations. This just does not happen today.

I hope I have enlightened you as the reader in some way. If you have children who are currently in the grades of pre-k to twelfth grade, I hope you have realized your children's education and their involvement in extracurricular activities should not be a financial burden for you. Our tax dollars are collected to pay for our children's education. Our tax dollars should not be distributed to private sources that do not deserve the money. The responsibility of funding a solid, all-around education to our children belongs to our federal, state, and local governments. It is our politicians who have their priorities in the wrong order. We have to reestablish to our politicians the importance of educating our children to be strong, independent thinkers. This is why we must place in office individuals who are not already bought and paid for by other interests.